Liberation Pedagogy

Liberation Pedagogy

Elijah Muhammad and the Art of Soul Crafting

Abul Pitre

ROWMAN & LITTLEFIELD
Lanham • Boulder • New York • London

Published by Rowman & Littlefield
An imprint of The Rowman & Littlefield Publishing Group, Inc.
4501 Forbes Boulevard, Suite 200, Lanham, Maryland 20706
www.rowman.com

86-90 Paul Street, London EC2A 4NE

British Library Cataloguing in Publication Information Available

Library of Congress Cataloging-in-Publication Data

ames: Pitre, Abul, author.
Title: Liberation pedagogy : Elijah Muhammad and the art of soul crafting /
    Abul Pitre.
Description: Lanham : Rowman & Littlefield, [2022] | Includes
    bibliographical references and index. | Summary: "Liberation Pedagogy
    places the work of Elijah Muhammad in an educational context. Drawing
    from concepts in critical educational theory it introduces to readers
    the contributions that Elijah Muhammad made to the education of
    oppressed people. This book offers a liberation pedagogy that educators
    can use to inspire students"— Provided by publisher.
Identifiers: LCCN 2022009273 (print) | LCCN 2022009274 (ebook) | ISBN
    9781475865417 (cloth) | ISBN 9781475865424 (paperback) | ISBN
    9781475865431 (epub)
Subjects: LCSH: Critical pedagogy. | Liberation theology. | Elijah Muhammad,
    1897–1975—Philosophy. | African Americans—Education—Philosophy. |
    Social justice and education. | Minorities—Education—Philosophy.
Classification: LCC LC196 .P587 2022 (print) | LCC LC196 (ebook) | DDC
    370.11/5—dc23/eng/20220512
LC record available at https://lccn.loc.gov/2022009273
LC ebook record available at https://lccn.loc.gov/2022009274

Dedicated to Harold Muhammad, Tynnetta Muhammad,
James Conyers, and Abdulalim Shabazz.

You will forever be remembered!

Contents

Preface

This book was started nearly thirty years ago when the author was first introduced to the teachings of Elijah Muhammad. As a new high school social studies teacher in a predominantly Black school, he wanted to empower students to become transformative leaders who would positively impact their local communities. To reach students, he connected the academic content to the students' lived reality. He was unknowingly using the tenets of culturally relevant pedagogy, which entails both helping students to achieve academic success using each student's culture to support their learning of academic content and helping students to become critically conscious.

The school where he taught was plagued with territorial fights. The gangster images from the movie *Colors*, along with images from rap videos that depicted Black males smoking marijuana and drinking gin and juice, were deeply sketched in his students' minds.

Concerned with the violence that was taking place in the school, he volunteered to hold discussion sessions with the Black male students who were beefing with each other. Knowing very little about African American studies, he began framing the discourse for these students around Black history.

The study of Black history started to make these students conscious of the social inequities in the school and in communities they lived in. They began to ask questions. Why did their White teachers refer to them as "jungle bunnies"? Why did Black people live on the poor side of the railroad tracks while Whites lived in better neighborhoods? Carter G.

Woodson's (1999) writing was brought to life as they began to realize how the present reality had been shaped by past events.

The author was later asked by the principal to lead the organization of the school's Black history program. He met with the student council to find out their ideas for the program. They chimed, "We are tired of having a dream. How long will it take before *we shall overcome*?" With passion, they declared that they wanted someone like Malcolm X. The author searched everywhere for what he called "Nation of Islam people" and was fortunate to be put in touch with a minister from New Orleans.

We couldn't afford an honorarium, only payment for gas, food, and a hotel room. The night before the Black history program, the parents, the students, and the author had dinner with the speaker. The things he was saying about Black history left the author speechless. He thought, *I have a degree in history and don't know any of the things he's teaching about.*

The Black history program was a huge success. The Black male students were in tears and vowed to no longer fight one another. The community leaders were overjoyed to the degree that they could not believe the power of Black history to redirect the lives of Black students. The next day, the news media, sheriff's deputies, and central office administrators converged on the school. They had learned from a White teacher that there would be violence because of a speech given by a *Black Muslim*. When they arrived on campus, they wanted to meet with the author because he organized the Black history program. He was a football coach who was doing well in supplying the White high school coach with exceptional football players.

The central office administrators asked him one question: Would you do the Black history program the same way? His reply was yes. They ended the meeting with no further questions, but over the next year they were determined to make the author pay a price for raising the consciousness of Black students.

While they sought to do many things that placed his life in danger, he wanted to know more about the teachings of Elijah Muhammad. Prior to knowing anything about Elijah Muhammad, he had used tapes of Malcolm X in his class and wondered why Elijah Muhammad didn't sit down and be quiet.

The more he read Elijah Muhammad's books and the more they planned to do him harm, Elijah Muhammad became his personal guide to understanding his teachings. Over time, the two of them became *blood brothers*. When they finally removed him from the school, he had become an avid reader. The community was in an uproar over his transfer to another school, and it sparked community protests, with a local pastor leading the charge.

The author would later decide to pursue a doctoral degree in education. After completing the degree, he began his academic career in a unique master's program in urban education, which was conceptually driven by *critical pedagogy*, and he was shocked to see how the writings of critical pedagogues were similar to the teachings of Elijah Muhammad.

He began to see that at the core of Elijah Muhammad's mission was the dissemination of a *Supreme Wisdom*. It became more apparent to him that Elijah Muhammad was an *Educator*, a *Divine Teacher*, and *Messenger* in the wilderness of North America. As the author pondered over the many writings about Elijah Muhammad, he began to realize that many people disliked him because of a negative propaganda campaign that was orchestrated by those in high places. Elijah Muhammad was labeled a racist and a mad man, said not to be a real Muslim, and called other names that are too foul to restate. Not only was he the target of false propaganda, but also his teachings were not examined by educators, despite his ability to reeducate Blacks on the lowest social stratum. Over the years, the author began to see Elijah Muhammad as a precursor to critical pedagogy. Thus, this book's title became *Liberation Pedagogy: Elijah Muhammad and the Art of Soul Crafting*.

This book was originally intended to be a short reader titled *Elijah Muhammad and Education*, but it got reshaped as the author read more about his subject. The author had in his possession for over twenty-three years Claude Clegg's (1997) book *An Original Man: The Life and Times of Elijah Muhammad* but couldn't bring himself to read it. Once he accepted a position to chair the famed Department of Africana Studies at San Francisco State University and received approval to teach the course "The Life and Thought of Elijah Muhammad," he read Clegg's book in a few days. Clegg's book made him more aware of the many trials and tribulations Elijah Muhammad faced because he sought to liberate Black people. The author had now begun to realize the deep love that Elijah Muhammad had for those languishing under oppression.

The global pandemic, the murder of Black people, and the climate changes that are occurring caused the author to see the urgency in writing this book. Elijah Muhammad (1973)—in his book *The Fall of America*—spoke of similar events, and this fueled the author's desire to write this book. The little man from rural Georgia holds the keys to a body of knowledge that will give birth to a new world. His teachings touched the soul of his students, tapping their divine essence. The souls of people like Malcolm X, Warith D. Mohammed, Muhammad Ali, and Louis Farrakhan were touched, causing them to speak truth to power. Through a reeducation program, Elijah Muhammad brought a new culture to Blacks in America.

BLOOD BROTHERS

The controversial Black history program that was mentioned earlier led the author to have personal experiences with Elijah Muhammad. They were beautiful encounters in tranquil settings. When he reflects on these encounters, the author is reminded of how his view of Elijah Muhammad was distorted. In the author's schooling, he had heard about Malcolm X but never listened to an entire speech by him. He only watched small clips of Malcolm speaking, and in complete ignorance, when he first heard Elijah Muhammad speak, thought to himself, *He needs to sit down and let Malcolm talk.* Like most people, the author was clueless about Elijah Muhammad's teachings but joined the herd who had swallowed the propaganda that hid the streams of knowledge he possessed.

Nevertheless, as he began to study Elijah Muhammad's teachings while referencing other books to draw conclusions, he became enthralled to the degree that he could not put his study of these teachings down. These teachings quarantined him, leaving him with no desire to leave home. The controversy around the Black history program and his work among the students had put his life in danger. This caused him to read more intensely, and before he knew it, he was encountering this legendary figure in ways that were incomprehensible to him.

This legendary figure had now sat beside him, becoming his personal guide to understanding his teachings. Traveling in the wilderness of his home community, he encountered other people who knew Elijah Muhammad intimately but were quiet about this relationship. One example was a much older lady whose home was in the middle of a field but visible from a major highway that ran through the area. The author was told to visit with her by a former student who had completed some handiwork at her home.

The author would never have imagined that this elderly woman in the backwoods of Louisiana knew about the teachings of Elijah Muhammad. Her words still resonate with him: "That old man is going to jump in you." It is through this context that the author writes about Elijah Muhammad's liberation pedagogy and the art of soul crafting.

When the author encountered the literature on multicultural education (Banks, 2019), critical pedagogy (Freire, 2018), critical race theory (CRT) (Ladson-Billings & Tate, 1995), and Whiteness studies (Clark & O'Donnell, 1999), he saw the underpinnings of Elijah Muhammad's teachings. This line of research has been viewed with skepticism by colleagues in the colleges of education where he has worked, with the exception of a few universities.

The name Elijah Muhammad is frightening to educators, even those from historically marginalized groups, because many of them have a fear of freedom (Freire, 2018). During his tenure at historically Black colleges and universities, many would argue that professors of education should stick to the rules and traditions of preparing technicians, not critical intellectuals who would advocate for those languishing in oppressive school environments. To these professors, education is apolitical. This book seeks to expand on the author's earlier works on Elijah Muhammad to provide laypersons, educators, and future educators with a greater understanding of how his teachings can radically transform schools and society.

MORE ABOUT THE BOOK

Chapter 1, "Spirituality, Education, and Black Liberation Theology," introduces the teachings of Elijah Muhammad by placing his life's mission in a spiritual context. Muhammad was regarded by many as a *Messenger of God* commissioned to spiritually awaken Blacks in America, and his work was rooted in education. The chapter also examines teacher education, arguing that the study of critical Black pedagogues is absent in educator-preparation programs. The chapter introduces educators to *Black liberation theology* in the context of Elijah Muhammad's teachings. The section on Black liberation theology highlights that the education of Blacks in America is connected to the visitation of the Supreme Being to liberate Black and other oppressed people. The chapter concludes with a discussion of Elijah Muhammad's contribution to the discipline of education.

Chapter 2, "The Writers, Islam, and Social Justice," discusses some of the well-known books and journals about the Nation of Islam and Elijah Muhammad. It also explores how Elijah Muhammad is excluded from the educational discourse because he was a Muslim. The chapter discusses how most educators are Christian and as a result may not have interest in the study of Elijah Muhammad's teachings. A highlight of the chapter is Chrislam, which is the merging of Christianity and Islam. In discussing Chrislam, the chapter argues that the Nation of Islam reflects the merging of Christianity and Islam.

Chapter 3, "Humble Beginnings," begins with a discussion of the need for educators to have historical knowledge. This historical knowledge should include information about the multicultural histories of the diversity of people living in America. As such, the chapter briefly discusses how education has been used as a tool to domesticate historically underserved groups (Freire, 2018; Spring, 2016). It explores the teachings of Elijah Muhammad relating to the ancient history of Black people. Additionally, the chapter provides a brief biographical account of how Elijah Poole, the son of sharecroppers in rural Georgia, became Elijah Muhammad, the leader of the Nation of Islam, one of the most powerful Black organizations in American history.

Chapter 4, "The Teachings," explores Elijah Muhammad's teachings in the context of critical pedagogy, critical race theory, and critical Whiteness studies. Elijah Muhammad saw his mission as one that would empower Blacks to do for themselves. Like critical pedagogues, he believed those in the dominating group would not provide the requisite knowledge to free Blacks in America. In exploring critical race theory, the chapter argues that CRT is an offshoot of Elijah Muhammad's teachings (Abdullah, 2016). Derek Bell, the father of CRT, was influenced by Malcolm X, an advocate of Black nationalism, and a pupil of Elijah Muhammad (Delgado & Stefancic, 2017). The chapter connects the teachings of Elijah Muhammad with critical Whiteness studies, a relatively new topic of discussion in the field of education (Leonardo, 2009).

Chapter 5, "Soul Crafting," places the work of Elijah Muhammad in a spiritual context. Drawing from Cornel West's position that education is soul crafting, it discusses Elijah Muhammad's most notable pupils: Minister Malcolm X, Imam Warith D. Mohammed, Muhammad Ali, and Minister Louis Farrakhan. Soul crafting for Elijah Muhammad was more than frank or bold speech; it was the awakening of the divine essence resonating in the human being. Blacks who were dead to their innate powers took on new life through the acquisition of supreme wisdom they received from Elijah Muhammad.

Included in the chapter is a discussion of the role of the woman in the education process. The chapter also discusses Elijah Muhammad's teaching about the role of food and places it in an educational context, arguing that the eating of food is also spiritual in that it means digesting certain bodies of knowledge. Soul crafting epitomized the personal transformation that took place in Elijah Muhammad's life and was extended to the many persons who were influenced by his teaching.

In this book, you will read how Elijah Muhammad's teachings contribute to the disciplines of education and Africana studies. We hope this book will touch your soul!

Chapter One

Spirituality, Education, and Black Liberation Theology

The discipline of education is often perceived from a technical aspect and includes the development of lesson plans, teaching methods, and assessment. In the twenty-first century, lesson plans are prepackaged to the degree that teachers are required to follow pacing guides. The push toward a common core curriculum has also played a role in the preparation of teachers.

McLaren (2015) posited that teachers have been reduced to technicians. William Pinar (2020) wrote that teachers have become mail carriers for politicians. Seen from this perspective, education in the twenty-first century has continued to serve the purpose of domesticating students (Freire, 2018). In contrast to the domesticating function of education are liberation pedagogies.

For people of African descent, education also entails the spiritual. Elijah Muhammad's work among Black people was a spiritual undertaking, and his view of education was rooted in theological discourse. When he advocated that Blacks gain the knowledge of self, this meant they would discover their unique gifts and talents.

Beyond advocating, Elijah Muhammad was engaged in the act of teaching Blacks the knowledge of self. For example, when taught about the origin of all life that exists, he created a hunger in Black people to seek knowledge. This chapter explores Elijah Muhammad's teachings regarding the ways education embodies a spiritual component. It highlights Black liberation theology and argues that this should be studied by preservice and in-service teachers.

LIBERATION AND EDUCATION

For over forty-four years, Elijah Muhammad labored to free Blacks in America from the oppression they experienced. He didn't use carnal weapons but believed it was knowledge that Blacks needed to attain freedom. When he met his teacher, Wallace D. Fard, he was ignorant of the four pillars of knowledge, which include *the knowledge of self, the knowledge of God, the knowledge of the devil,* and *the knowledge of time.* As an *ummi* (unlearned person), he was ignorant of the divine essence resonating in him.

He was like the masses of students in public schools wandering aimlessly in life. Under the foot of a dominant Western-centric society, he was not conscious of how those ruling the society had purposefully hidden knowledge to maintain their rule over Black people. After studying under his teacher, Master Fard Muhammad, he emerged to become the *Messenger of Allah.* Equipped with a body of knowledge that would liberate Blacks in America, he suffered for over forty years because he sought to liberate them.

With only a fourth-grade education, he taught about the likes of Covid-19, climate change, the fight for racial justice, and fratricide. He was a *divine teacher* who believed there was a need for people to be raised into a spiritual consciousness that would lead to *liberation.* Liberation would entail freedom from the dominant Western-centric civilization, which had produced a culture that was based on fulfilling animalistic desires. The animalistic side of the human being operates from the reptilian brain, finding pleasure in things that feed the lower desires.

European scholar Abraham Maslow (1943) wrote about human needs and motivation. Maslow's pyramid of human needs stated that at the lowest level are material things such as food, clothing, and shelter. Whereas Maslow borrowed his ideas from the Blackfoot Native Americans, he didn't highlight their discourse around spirituality (Safir, 2020). Aboriginal peoples believed the spiritual embodied all aspects of human endeavor, in contrast to Europeans, who placed a high value on material possessions. In the Eurocentric world, people's labor for the ruling group allows them to obtain food, clothing, and shelter. To survive, people have to purchase these necessities from those who have taken the earth into their possession.

The Native Americans saw the earth as Mother because it produces all that is necessary for its inhabitants to survive. The arrival of Europeans to the Americas brought a new way of life that was the opposite of that of the aboriginal people. Europeans didn't see the earth as Mother; instead, they saw it as a material possession that they needed to take from the aboriginal owners. Thus, land theft has marked the long history of European dominance (G. Howard, 2006).

Wherever the earth has resources, Europeans have gained control of the resources and the people. Under European dominance, the earth and all its inhabitants have languished, longing to be free. The earth—burdened by the destruction it has experienced under European dominance—would one day give birth to a person anointed with a body of knowledge that, like the light, dispels darkness. This person would possess a superior knowledge that would be so great it would end oppression, suffering, and death.

In America, there would be a group of people who were kidnapped from their native lands. Enslaved in the Americas, these descendants of Africa were stripped of their languages, cultures, names, and religions (Karenga, 2002). At the end of dominant Western-centric rule on the planet, the Supreme Being would travel the earth to find these *lost members* of his family who had been stripped of their ancestral knowledge. After finding them, he would teach one from among these despised and rejected people, making him a *Messenger* to those people.

The *Messenger* would possess the keys to a body of knowledge that could unlock the chains that had kept this particular people from knowing the treasures they embodied. Like the earth, which contains great mineral wealth, these African descendants who were once chattel slaves did not know that God resided in them. They were given the name *Negro* because they experienced mental death as a result of being stripped of the knowledge of self.

Under the yoke of European dominance, they would over time become spiritually dead. This in turn would cause them to become partakers of a culture that led to evil practices. Living under this type of culture, they would not be able to hear the inner voice: the voice of God that was asleep in them. The dominant Western-centric civilization would cause these African descendants to become partakers of sport and play, intoxicating drinks, tobacco, drugs, and illicit sex. These baser desires would lead to a degenerate culture that would lead to self-destructive behaviors.

After three hundred years of Black people serving as chattel slaves, the Whites who were designing their education would not seek to teach them of their ancestral history. And in organizing their education, these White architects would not seek to awaken the inner voice of Blacks but would instead drown it out. Today, the superrich use Black people's creative expression of their pain and suffering to produce a culture that is alien to them.

Through music and entertainment, the adversary of God uses his voice to lead the youth astray. The owners of the entertainment world engineer the youth to glory in being savage and the killing of their brethren. They unknowingly break all the commandments to relive the murder of Abel at the hands of his brother, Cain. Ignorant of the Holy Quran, which declares that the killing of one person is like the killing of all people, they make songs that glorify a bestial life.

They would need a divine teacher to make them conscious of things that rendered them spiritually dead. The more than three hundred years of chattel slavery that Blacks in America experienced would give birth to one of the former slaves who would meet God in person and, through the act of teaching, possess a body of knowledge that would touch the soul of Black people. The suffering of Black people gave birth to Elijah Poole, who would later undergo a spiritual awakening to become Elijah Muhammad.

Today Elijah Muhammad remains one of the most controversial figures in history. He has been locked out of education discourse despite his ability to transform the lives of people across race, social class, and gender. He shared a teaching over eighty years ago that left those dominating the society in awe. They had never heard such a teaching and became alarmed to such a degree that J. Edgar Hoover had his home bugged and infiltrated FBI agents into the Nation of Islam to destroy it. Elijah Muhammad was the most spied on of all Black leaders (Gardell, 1996).

To date he is still one of the most misunderstood Black leaders because of the spread of misinformation about him by those in high places. Those in high places fear the *light* of his teachings could free people from the oppressive systems that have locked away their human potential. His life and teachings give meaning to the words of Jesus, who declared, "You shall know the truth, and the truth shall set you free" (John 8:32 MEV). It is through *knowing* that human beings can be made free.

Elijah Muhammad pointed out that the knowledge of self, God, and the devil was the most important of all knowledge. Regarding Blacks in America, the greatest crime that those ruling the society made was robbing and depriving them of the knowledge of self. He went on to say anyone teaching Blacks the knowledge of self would face persecution. For over forty years, Elijah Muhammad lived his life on a cross, suffering ridicule, slander, and the threat of death because he was raising a people who had been placed in the bowels of society to become the cornerstone of a new civilization.

In the education world, there is widespread discourse about how to improve the educational outcomes of Black students. However, there is virtually no discussion among school leaders and teachers regarding who is determining those outcomes. Joel Spring (2011) wrote that education in America is premised on human capitalist economics, which is the belief that the primary function of school is to prepare a workforce. Under the guise of improving educational outcomes, high-stakes testing is used to label schools.

Predominantly Black schools might be labeled as F schools or poor-performing schools. Testing serves the purpose of giving the appearance that Black students are deficient. In the name of social justice, new gimmicks are sold to school districts that are supposed help them improve the educational outcomes of their students. Testing is big business, and it is a throwback to the eugenics movement, which was used to support the belief that Blacks were inferior. The ideology of human capitalist economics has put to death the gifts and talents of too many Black students.

When the world marveled at the eloquence of the brilliant Amanda Gorman, they perhaps did not know that in the dilapidated school buildings in urban America and wherever Black students are found, there is an abundance of talent that is left untapped. Unfortunately, schools are not designed to bring out that talent; nor were they created to liberate Black people. They have a long history of serving the interest of the powerful.

A review of educational history reveals how the White architects of Black education developed schools to serve their interest. William

Watkins (2001) wrote that these architects sought to use education to make Blacks submissive to White rule. Carter G. Woodson (1999) called this miseducation and decried how Blacks were being taught that their Blackness was a curse. Woodson (1999) pointed out that Blacks were being educated in White supremacy. He declared that the education Black people were receiving caused them to go to the back door, and if there was no back door, they would make one.

TEACHER EDUCATION

To effectively maintain oppressive rule, the process of selecting teachers has been under the control of those in high places. Future educators are trained in teacher-preparation programs that do not prepare them to bring out the gifts and talents of all students but rather teach them how to police and deposit information that deadens the spirit. Teacher-preparation programs may offer one or two courses that address teaching diverse students, but they rarely prepare teachers to be antiracist educators.

Ladson-Billings (2021) wrote, "Although many teacher education programs include some form of multicultural education, confronting issues of racism in a deliberately anti-racist framework is less common" (p. 179). Courses in teacher education do not cover Black thought leaders who are considered outside the mainstream discourse. Persons like Elijah Muhammad and Marcus Garvey would not be studied because education is not designed to truly empower Black and other historically underserved students. Future teachers are highly likely to be trained to practice a *pedagogy of oppression*.

Prospective teachers, like students in K-12 schools, are required to take multiple-choice exams that do not get at the heart of what it means to teach. Licensure exams have become the tool used to eliminate prospective non-White teachers from pursuing a career in education. The intention of those ruling the society is to use nice language about the need to prepare more quality teachers, while the underlying goal appears to be hiring more teachers who hold Eurocentric perspectives. Trained in teacher-education programs that have a long history of racism and colorblindness, future teachers are not able to discern the matrix that has made too many educators into overseers of oppressive schools.

Through Eurocentric licensure processes, non-White teachers are being pushed out of the teaching force, making it a profession of majority White, female teachers. White teachers unfamiliar with the culture of non-White students might see these students as deficient. Moreover, White teachers may unknowingly have dysconscious racism, which could make it difficult for them to effectively teach non-White students (King, 2015).

A good example of this was when a White teacher at a majority Black school confronted a Black high school student about wearing a Black Lives Matter hoodie (Zeringue, 2019). The teacher told the student she would have to take the shirt off, to which the student replied she had permission to wear it. The White teacher then proceeded to physically remove the shirt from the student. Even though the teacher was charged with assault, it is another example of how White privilege *trumps* treating Black students with respect and dignity.

Not only do Black students face hostile White teachers, but they also sometimes encounter Black educators who are trained to hate everything Black. Woodson (1999) was insightful when he said that some Black educators were figureheads and defenders of a system that works to keep Black people oppressed.

Teacher-preparation programs play an important role in preparing educators who are not conscious that they can work to either liberate or domesticate students. The body of knowledge that educators are exposed to does not make them politically conscious. And even in cases where teacher-preparation programs attempt to address issues of equity and social justice, they might encounter students who are combative and resistant to discourse around these topics.

BLACK LIBERATION THEOLOGY

To understand the power of education, one has to place it in the context of theology. Theology is a science of the study of God. James Cone, the father of Black liberation theology, throughout his writings on the subject perhaps unknowingly described the work of Elijah Muhammad and his teacher, Master Fard Muhammad.

For example, in defining Christian theology as a theology of liberation, he wrote, "It is a rational study of the being of God in the world in light of the existential situation of the oppressed community, relating the forces of liberation to the essence of the gospel, which is *Jesus Christ*" (Cone, 2010, p. 1). He then discussed Yahweh's role in delivering the children of Israel from the oppression they experienced. Cone (2010) went further, writing that God took the form of Jesus, who is the *Oppressed One*.

He articulated that God is on the side of the oppressed Blacks in America. With regard to the role of Black liberation theology to the Black community, he acknowledged its pioneers:

> To try to separate Black Liberation from black religion is a mistake, because Black religion is authentic only when it is identified with the struggle for Black freedom. The influence of Marcus Garvey, Elijah Muhammad, Malcolm X, and Martin Luther King Jr., demonstrates the role of religion in the Black community. (Cone, 2010, p. 62)

A study of the life and teachings of Elijah Muhammad reveals that it is knowledge that liberates the oppressed. This means that the liberation of Black people is tied to the knowledge they acquire. As Malcolm X pointed out, "Education is an important element in the struggle for human rights. It is the means to help our children and our people rediscover their identity and thereby increase their self-respect. Education becomes the passport to the future" (Turner, 2019).

To place Black education in the context of theology is to understand the role of God in liberating oppressed people. The liberation of Blacks in America begins with them receiving literature that spiritually awakens them. In this sense, it could be argued that the entire system of education is designed to keep Black people from knowing the great secret that God has visited America to free them from the oppression they are experiencing under dominant Western-centric rule. Cone (2010) cogently said, "God comes to those who have been enslaved and abused and declares total identification with their situation, disclosing to them the rightness of their emancipation in their own terms" (p. 48).

In line with Cone's analysis, the visit of God to America would give birth to a *Messenger* who would be sent to teach the oppressed—Blacks in America—the knowledge of themselves. This knowledge would raise them into new forms of consciousness, leading them to become a new people. Cone (2010) wrote, "Knowing God means being on the side of the oppressed" (p. 69).

In America, the place where chattel slavery existed, a little Black man from rural Georgia was raised from his grave of ignorance and bequeathed a body of knowledge to lift not only Blacks in America but also the whole of humanity to higher levels of spiritual consciousness.

Elijah Muhammad was hated because he taught that God had visited America to free Blacks from their slave masters, and in that visit God taught him a body of knowledge that would raise Blacks in America from a dead level to one where their divine essence would be raised. Like Woodson and other critical Black pedagogues, Elijah Muhammad was critical of the Eurocentric education that Blacks were receiving.

When referring to the education of Black people, he said, "Momma may have and Poppa may have but God blesses the child who has his own" (Muhammad, 1965, p. 40). He was expressing the need for Black people to develop their own education system. He declared if a man won't treat you right, he won't teach you right.

Far beyond being critical, he offered a pedagogy of liberation that touched the souls of his students. For Elijah Muhammad, education was soul crafting. He taught that the wisdom of God lives in human beings (Muhammad, 1974). Blacks in America would need teachers who could teach them the knowledge of self (Muhammad, 1965).

Before him, W. E. B. Du Bois wrote that education is the drawing out of human powers (Aptheker & Du Bois, 1973). For Elijah Muhammad, knowledge was like water, and when it rained on students, it brought to life their mental powers. The light embodied in *Supreme Wisdom* would enliven them to the degree that through the power of thought, there would be a change in their physical appearance. He wrote,

> As you notice, the effect of thoughts or your thinking at times has such deep effect on the brain that it affects the surface of your face, skin, and body. Your eyes are also affected by that tremendous thought or way of thinking that you have as it acts upon your brain. (Muhammad, 1974, p. 124)

Elijah Muhammad is speaking to power of thought, which is not discussed in educator-preparation programs, *via teacher education or educational leadership*. More so, this aspect of his teachings is similar to neurotheology, an emerging area of study that explores the impact of theology on the brain. In *The Principles of Neurotheology*, Andrew Newberg (2010) wrote, "'Neurotheology' is a unique field of scholarship and investigation that seeks to understand the relationship specifically between the brain and theology, and more broadly between the mind and religion" (p. 1).

As early as the 1930s, Elijah Muhammad was teaching about the five brains. The five brains in modern terms are the five hemispheres of the brain. Before Black liberation theology discourse, he said that God, in the person of Master Fard Muhammad, had showered "his rays of the light of Love, Wisdom, Freedom, Justice and Equality through our frozen and dead sleeping seven and one-half ounces of our mental power, which is called our Five Senses or Brains" (E. Muhammad, 2012, p. 1).

The seven and one-half ounces that he is describing are the brain, and the rays of light are a body of knowledge that is grounded in the knowledge of God and self. Elijah Muhammad understood the power of thought, and this caused him to see how the enemies of Black liberation could weaponize the thoughts of people by way of social engineering.

The weaponization of thought would require knowing how those in power have used silent weapons (Cooper, 2019) to normalize actions that are designed to keep Black people from discovering their divine essence. The constant bombardment of negative images of Black people on TV and radio is an example of the use of silent weapons on the mind.

Elijah Muhammad (2006), in his monumental lecture "The Theology of Time," said, "He doesn't invite you to anything righteous. He invites you to evil. They play all evil and filthy music day and night to attract your attention" (pp. 331–332). In that same lecture series, he discussed the power of thought and how cleaning up the human faculties empowers people. There is a power in the human being that has to be activated. When Elijah Muhammad declared the wisdom of God lives in the human being, he was restating the words of Jesus, who told his disciples, "The kingdom of God is within you" (Luke 17:21 KJV).

The teacher, when properly educated, can bring out that kingdom. The current educational system is not premised on the goal of bringing out the talents and gifts for the majority of students, particularly Black students. The powerful, through their selection of knowledge used in schools and universities, have been able to maintain their rule by not providing the oppressed with the requisite knowledge that leads to freedom: *knowledge of self.*

Elijah Muhammad (1965) wrote, "No one can enslave another who has equal education" (p. 45). Cone (2010) reiterated that in Black liberation theology, "Revelation is self-knowledge, a knowledge in which human beings make a decision about their own existence in the world" (p. 56). In part, the education of the oppressed does not include the development of a spiritual consciousness. Black liberation theology, like multicultural education, should be infused into teacher-education programs because *the teacher*, knowingly or unknowingly, touches the souls of people.

Elijah Muhammad prepared ministers in every major city to teach and inspire Black people. He knew the value of preparing teachers who were dedicated to the liberation of Black and other oppressed people. In the early 1970s, he set up a teachers' college in Sedalia, North Carolina, and in the *Supreme Wisdom* lessons alluded to the preparation of a particular type of teacher to liberate the human family.

In the *Supreme Wisdom* teachings, he talks about the *Five Percent*, whom he declares are the poor righteous teachers who do not believe in a spook God but instead "teach Freedom, Justice, and Equality to all the human family of the planet earth" (E. Muhammad, 1993c, p. 19). Today there is a group of hip-hop artists who refer to themselves as the Five Percenters. The Five Percenters share some of the teachings of Elijah Muhammad with youth in the street.

The Five Percenters were founded by Clarence 13X, who decided to leave the physical building where the Nation of Islam held its meetings to share the teachings of Elijah Muhammad with youth in the streets of America (Allah, 2007). The Five Percenters reflect subaltern education, in contrast to the dominant education in schools. Preparing Five Percent teachers for K-12 schools means they need to be immersed in the teachings of Elijah Muhammad and Africana studies.

Africana studies would help educators explore the ancient history of Africana people prior to European colonization. This is in part why Elijah Muhammad argued that Black History Month was insufficient, because it primarily taught about the accomplishments of Black people in America for the benefit of their oppressors (Muhammad, 1965). In addition, content educators would learn what it means to educate from an African-centered perspective (Asante, 1991).

Educators in the twenty-first century need to be equipped with a body of knowledge that excites, inspires, and gives birth to a spiritual civilization. Elijah Muhammad envisioned people in that civilization being courteous to one another and committed to doing good to the whole of humanity.

CONTRIBUTION TO EDUCATION

Elijah Muhammad's contribution to the field of education is unknown to educators, even though his reeducation program transformed the lives of countless people and catapulted persons like Malcolm X, Warith D. Mohammed, Muhammad Ali, and Louis Farrakhan to world prominence. Whereas most people view him as a religious figure, he was foremost a teacher with great foresight.

In his book *The Fall of America*, he describes world events like COVID-19 and the untimely deaths of Black men at the hands of police officers (E. Muhammad, 1973). (In *The Fall of America*, also see Chapter 54, titled "The Calamity," in which he discusses chemical bacteriologists who are polluting the water and air. The book also discusses the police brutality that Black men are experiencing.) Moreover, his teachings continue to have a transforming effect on people across various races, ethnicities, and social classes.

Elijah Muhammad is an anomaly to educators even though his great commission was grounded in education. His teachings inspired a whole population of people to seek knowledge. Moreover, he brought a whole new culture to Blacks in America that distinguished them from the American populace. The knowledge emanating from him has never been disclosed to those pursuing a career in education. His profound teachings covered everything from the origins of life to the foods one should eat (E. Muhammad, 1965, 1967, 1973, 1974).

With all the educational rhetoric around diversity, equity, critical pedagogy, and social justice, he was a forerunner of these modern constructs. Despite these accomplishments, there are no special interest groups in his name at major conferences such as the American Education Research Association, and most people know more about his students (Berg, 2009). With only a fourth-grade education, he built an entire nation for Blacks in America.

To take a people who were less than seventy years removed from chattel slavery and banned from reading for over two hundred years to produce a new civilization was miraculous. The entire work of Elijah Muhammad was educational (Pitre, 2015). His teachings covered all the disciplines and fields of study found in major research universities (Pitre, 2021b). One could even argue that his teachings have sparked the modern advancements we are experiencing in the disciplines and fields of study in modern education.

With regard to education, he not only offered a critical pedagogical language but also started schools in the urban centers of America for the reeducation of Blacks in the country. These schools at the onset faced persecution from the dominant governing structure, which feared his teachings would lead to revolution and liberation (E. Muhammad, 1965). As a result, he was arrested for his refusal to send Muslim students to public schools and instead enrolling them in Muhammad University of Islam (E. Muhammad, 1965).

Unlike civil rights leaders, who were seeking to integrate into the mainstream of American society, he espoused separation. His teachings disclosed the underlying ideological foundations that kept Black people from reaching their full potential. When Malcolm X talked about Blacks not coming to America on the *Mayflower* and said that they were not part of the landing on Plymouth Rock, but rather that Plymouth Rock had landed on Blacks, this raised their consciousness (Breitman, 1965).

Malcolm was using the teachings that he received from Elijah Muhammad to awaken Blacks to the oppressor consciousness that caused them to be dependent on their former *slave masters*. The many books that have rightfully expressed the greatness of Malcolm X never mentioned that as an eighth-grade school dropout with a criminal record, he would never have been allowed to attend elite high schools and would not have been admitted to lower-tier universities.

It was the teachings of Elijah Muhammad and the platform he provided for Malcolm that allowed his brilliance to come forth. Elijah Muhammad epitomized the *art of soul crafting* through education by bringing out the talents and gifts in his students (Pitre, 2015). The false narratives about Elijah Muhammad have been intentional because his teachings lead to complete freedom.

In the field of education, the discourse around racism, Whiteness, and social justice—among many more topics—has similarities to his teachings. For example, he had been teaching about freedom, justice, and equality in the 1930s, and this was one of the key tenets of the Nation of Islam. Unlike those who are jumping on the rhetoric of social justice, Elijah Muhammad (1973) taught about *equal justice*.

With only a fourth-grade education, he wrote, "Justice is a common thing. Yet, it is elusive. Men have sought its meaning since time began. Plato shrugged that justice was nothing more than the wish of the strongest members of society" (E. Muhammad, 1973, p. 2). He went on to describe justice as the antithesis of wrong:

> Jesus equated justice with brotherhood. Shakespeare saw it as a matter of mercy. I am here to tell you that justice is the eventual working out of the will of God as indicated in the fundamental principles of truth. Justice is the antithesis of wrong, the weapon God will use to bring judgment upon the world, the purpose and consummation of his coming (E. Muhammad, 1973, p. 2).

With a very limited Eurocentric education, coming out of the cotton fields of Georgia, just out of chattel slavery, he offered a definitive understanding of justice grounded in theological discourse.

The social justice movement, with its many educators, has failed to mention Elijah Muhammad, and when his name is brought up, many of these social justice advocates are alarmed. It makes one wonder if they are truly working in the best interest of oppressed groups. Elijah Muhammad's teachings offer a model that could be used to radically transform educational practice.

This radical transformation of educational practice will not necessarily occur completely in the traditional school setting, because as Apple (2019) contended, schools are doing what they were designed to do: maintain the social hierarchy. In spite of this, the teachings of Elijah Muhammad, when properly understood, can be a tool for educators.

This book intends to place the teachings of Elijah Muhammad within the educational discourse. The name Muhammad and the word "Islam" may cause trepidation for educators. The majority of educators may reject his insights, but this is not unusual considering the same fate was experienced by prophets, messengers, and great teachers who proceeded him. Socrates is but one example of a teacher who was in opposition to the rulers of his day. For his truth telling, he was put to death for making the youth conscious.

Another challenge in studying Elijah Muhammad is that most educators are Christian and overcoming the oft-repeated lie that Muslims don't believe in Jesus might be daunting. Islam is not new in America, and it has been studied by people like George Washington, Thomas Jefferson, and other American leaders in secret societies like the Masons (Pitre, 2016). The knowledge that Elijah Muhammad disclosed, when carefully studied, is a light that awakens the power of one's inner self. It is soul crafting!

CONCLUSION

Elijah Muhammad not only offered a critique of Black education but also developed universities throughout urban America. These universities were specifically created to meet the needs of the Muslim community under his leadership. By setting up these universities, he was offering a model of what could happen when Black students were placed in environments where teachers had high expectations and knew the cultural context of their students.

In addition to knowing the cultural context, teachers would need to be equipped with a body of knowledge that would inspire and cultivate the genius in students. They would be in love with Black people and committed to their liberation.

The teachings of Elijah Muhammad offer a Black liberation theology of education that could awaken Black consciousness. This would grow Black people into discovering their relationship with the creator and stimulate their creative mind. As opposed to viewing their Blackness as a curse, they would learn that the universe came to exist through the Originator, the Black man.

In the context of Black liberation theology, if God is to liberate the oppressed, he brings a body of knowledge that will set them free from the ideologies that have enslaved them. The education of Black people in the context of Black liberation theology means that their education is a national security threat.

In the 1960s, the threat of Black intelligence led to a *counterintelligence* program that sought to eliminate Black consciousness. Today, termed *Black identity extremists*, those who advocate for freedom, justice, and equality for African descendants may find themselves surveilled, harassed, imprisoned, or dead (Brown, 2021; Darah, 2018).

Elijah Muhammad offered a spiritual toolkit that could eradicate the diseases that were impacting the human family. When he taught about the power of thought and the five brains, he was preparing people for future discourses in spiritual matters. He was a forerunner of many leading theoretical models premised on social justice.

Chapter Two

The Writers, Islam, and Social Justice

The name Elijah Muhammad conjures many thoughts and opinions. To his older followers, he is the beloved *Messenger of Allah* and to a new generation of followers the exalted Christ. And then there are those who see him as a false prophet, a hate teacher (Pipes, 2000), and the man responsible for the death of Malcolm X. There are several books about him; however, the majority have been written through the lens of history, political science, sociology, and religious studies (Berg, 2009; Clegg, 1997; Curtis, 2006; Evanzz, 2001; Lincoln, 1963; Muhammad-Ali, 2002; Essien-Udom, 1962; Walker, 2005).

This chapter highlights some of the well-known books and articles about Elijah Muhammad and the Nation of Islam. It critiques these works, arguing that some of them have been skewed as a result of limitations in establishing trustworthiness and credibility (a part of qualitative research) or have been written with the intent to disparage Elijah Muhammad. To disclose to readers the author's personal bias, the preface of this book notes how he became interested in studying Elijah Muhammad.

In addition, this chapter briefly discusses Islam in the context of education, highlighting how the field is dominated by teacher educators who are Christian. As a result, Elijah Muhammad is not mentioned in education discourse, even though many of the theoretical constructs in education that are centered around equity, race, and social justice have similarities to his teachings.

This chapter also discusses Elijah Muhammad's teachings about the origin of Black people and contends that teacher-education professors and preservice teacher candidates are not exposed to the ancient history of Black people that predates European civilization. The chapter concludes with a brief critique of social justice, arguing that those rallying around the term should pay homage to critical Black educators who paved the way for social justice discourse.

POPULAR WORKS ABOUT ELIJAH MUHAMMAD

This section explores some of the popular books and articles about Elijah Muhammad and the Nation of Islam. It highlights single-author books, the first journal article on the Nation of Islam, a TV documentary, and recently edited books on the Nation of Islam. This section is not an exhaustive exploration of books and articles but is used to highlight some of the original works that became the groundwork for future studies on the Nation of Islam and Elijah Muhammad. It also highlights newer works that pave the way for renewed discourse about the implications of Elijah Muhammad's teachings in the twenty-first century.

In 1997, Claude Clegg published *An Original Man: The Life and Times of Elijah Muhammad*. The book was very detailed, covering a wide range of historical pieces about Elijah Muhammad. It discussed his teachings, highlighted key figures in the Nation of Islam, provided information related to the assassination of Malcolm X, and discussed the Nation of Islam after the death of Elijah Muhammad.

Another well-known book is *The Messenger: The Rise and Fall of Elijah Muhammad* by Karl Evanzz (2001). Written like a fictional story, it raises questions around the accuracy of many of the claims about the life story of Elijah Muhammad. A gifted writer, Evanzz draws readers into the book, causing them to crave more. Unfortunately, there was falsehood mixed with truth that only Nation of Islam followers with experiences around the events he discussed or those immersed in the study of the group would be able to clarify.

The book is not balanced or objective but was written to defame Elijah Muhammad. To those familiar with the history of Elijah Muhammad and the Nation of Islam, several of Evanzz's claims are questionable.

One example is Evanzz's claim that FBI documents substantiate that the founder of the Nation of Islam was a con man arrested on drug charges whose real name was Wallace Dodd. Wesley Muhammad (2019) refuted these claims, arguing that the 816-page FBI file does not confirm that Wallace Dodd is Wallace Fard. He then questioned Evanzz's authenticity, asking if he was a throwback to J. Edgar Hoover's counterintelligence program, which included writers who were intentionally trying to defame the Nation of Islam and its leader (Muhammad, 2019).

The earliest writing on the Nation of Islam is Edmond Beynon's 1938 "The Voodoo Cult among Negro Migrants in Detroit," which includes stories from interviews conducted with members in the Nation of Islam. Beynon does not provide readers with details of how this purportedly empirical study began or the protocols put in place to ensure the validity and trustworthiness of his findings. The name "voodoo cult" derives from his interpretation.

Beynon's study became the foundation for future studies on the Nation of Islam. In part, the term "cult" originated from the arrest of a so-called member of the Nation of Islam who committed a murder under the auspices of following the teachings in the *Supreme Wisdom* book. Nasir Hakim (1997) pointed out that this person was manipulated by a splinter group in an effort to thwart the spread of the Nation of Islam's teachings by way of Elijah Muhammad.

In 1951, Hatim Sahib completed a thesis titled "The Nation of Islam." The study used an ethnographic approach, which afforded him the opportunity to conduct an in-depth interview of Elijah Muhammad along with several of his followers. Sahib received permission from Elijah Muhammad to conduct the study, noting that Mr. Muhammad told his followers to be truthful in answering Sahib's questions (Sahib, 1951). The study was rich in terms of explaining how Elijah Muhammad met Wallace D. Fard, also known by Nation of Islam members as Master Fard Muhammad.

It also described the Nation of Islam's organizational structure and gathered stories of members' experiences. Sahib—borrowing Beynon's verbiage—also used the word "cult" to describe the Nation of Islam, a term that was not used by members to describe it. The study does not mention how the data was checked for credibility or trustworthiness. In using the term "cult," Sahib did not use verbiage that would be consistent with group members' self-identification.

Despite the magnificent contribution that Sahib's (1951) research added to the body of knowledge about the Nation of Islam, the terminology used to identify the group indicated that Sahib did not use member checking to enhance the trustworthiness and credibility of the study. To his credit, at the time of the study, many of the components that are currently used to conduct qualitative research were not available.

Essien-Udom's 1962 book *Black Nationalism: A Search for Identity in America* used an ethnographic approach to study the Nation of Islam. The book covers in great detail Elijah Muhammad's early beginnings and discloses the organization's early members along with its founder, Wallace D. Fard. A chapter titled "Education of Muslims" describes the purpose and function of the University of Islam. Moreover, the book provides intricate details about the Nation, dispelling many of the myths that have come to characterize the organization.

Curtis E. Lincoln (1963) conducted an ethnographic study in which he made note of his creation of the term "Black Muslims." Nation of Islam members never referred to themselves as Black Muslims, which demonstrates how scholars have infused their own biases when writing about them. Lincoln mentioned that many of those in Black intelligentsia would declare the teachings of Elijah Muhammad repugnant.

This is understandable considering that many intellectuals would have been schooled in a Eurocentric perspective (Woodson, 1999). Overall, Lincoln's work has some good information, but it does not capture the essence of the Nation's teachings. At the time that Lincoln's first edition was about to be published, the FBI had been exploring ways to curtail the growth of the Nation of Islam (Gardell, 1996).

In 1959, the documentary *The Hate That Hate Produced* (Wallace & Lomax, 1959) was designed to sway a national audience to see the Nation of Islam in a negative light. It was hoped that this propaganda would curb its growth and eventually lead to its demise. In addition, several articles (M. Y. Khan, 1959; Balk & Haley, 1963; Montgomery, 1963) were written in consonance with J. Edgar Hoover's counter-intelligence program. Even though most writings do not explore the teachings of Elijah Muhammad in any depth, some books attempt to be authentic in their examination.

Three of those books provide a wide range of information and include sources from the Nation of Islam (Gardell, 1996; Berg, 2009;

Pitre, 2015). In his book *In the Name of Elijah Muhammad: Louis Farrakhan and the Nation of Islam*, Gardell (1996) discloses that he is writing from the perspective of the Nation of Islam. He uses newspaper accounts, videos, and other sources to support his claims. Likewise, Herbert Berg (2009) writes with a different focus by exploring Elijah Muhammad through the lens of religious study. Berg painstakingly tries to understand Elijah Muhammad through scriptural interpretation. Pitre (2015) explores the work of Elijah Muhammad in an educational context, discussing his teachings through critical educational theory.

In addition, *New Perspectives on the Nation of Islam*, edited by Gibson and Berg (2016), discusses the Nation of Islam in a twenty-first-century context and covers a wide range of topics, like the *Muhammad Speaks* newspaper, culinary practices, and the Mother Wheel, among others. In *Africana Islamic Studies*, editors Conyers and Pitre (2016) offer a broad discussion about the Nation of Islam and Elijah Muhammad that includes diverse perspectives on the subject.

These studies—along with Bayinah Jeffries's 2014 *A Nation Can Rise No Higher Than Its Women: African American Muslim Women in the Movement for Black Self-Determination, 1950–1975* and Malachi Crawford's 2015 *Black Muslims and the Law: Civil Liberties from Elijah Muhammad to Muhammad Ali*—sparked the first research symposium on Elijah Muhammad studies.

In 2017, a group of scholars came together to share their research on some aspect of Elijah Muhammad. This body of diverse scholars included members of the Nation of Islam (S. Muhammad, 2003; R. Muhammad, 2013). The term "Elijah Muhammad studies" was coined by Pitre (2021a) in his book *An Introduction to Elijah Muhammad Studies*. The book outlines the interdisciplinary scope of Elijah Muhammad's teachings, arguing that many of the major research studies across disciplines are verifying his teachings.

Garrett Felber (2020), in his scholarly book *Those Who Know Don't Say: The Nation of Islam, the Black Freedom Movement, and the Carceral State*, documents the work of the Nation of Islam in the prisons of America. It documents the role the Nation of Islam played in advancing the rights of prisoners, describing the organization's work as the first prison litigation movement.

AN EDUCATION FOCUS

This book takes a different approach to understanding Elijah Muhammad, focusing entirely on education. It argues that the mission of Elijah Muhammad was reeducating Blacks in America. In reeducating Blacks in America, Muhammad's critiques disrupted the dominant ideology that contributed to White rule.

White supremacy for Elijah Muhammad was not about skin pigmentation but represented a way of being in the world; Whiteness was an ideology. While his message appeared in its early form to be directed to Blacks in America, it also brought to the consciousness of Whites the impact of their civilization on darker-skinned people throughout the world (Fardan, 2001; I. Hakim, n.d.).

In the twenty-first century, the field of education is undergoing a paradigm shift that is ushering in theoretical and conceptual frameworks that mirror Elijah Muhammad's teachings. Some of these include Afrocentricity, multicultural education, critical race theory, culturally relevant pedagogy, critical Whiteness studies, social justice education, and critical pedagogy. At several universities, educator-preparation programs are framed around these theoretical constructs.

Unfortunately, scholars in the field of education do not dare to mention Elijah Muhammad except for a few (Akom, 2003; Gollnick & Chinn, 2017; Ladson-Billings, 1995; Pinar, 2005; Pitre, 2010, 2015). This book is not intended to be a biography of Elijah Muhammad; nor does it attempt to provide a detailed history of the Nation of Islam's schools established in the 1930s. It is written to comparatively discuss Elijah Muhammad's teachings in relation to critical educational theory. Moreover, it seeks to introduce this great *master teacher* who has been locked out of the educational discourse because he has the keys to liberate those suffering under oppression.

ISLAM IN A CHRISTIAN WORLD

James Banks (2014), one of the leading scholars in multicultural education, pointed out that Islam is one of the fastest-growing religions in the United States, and most of its converts are African Americans. In his article "How Elijah Muhammad Won," Pipes (2000) writes that if the growth of Islam spreads among African Americans, the credit should go to Elijah Muhammad.

In the field of education, the study of diversity has included race, ethnicity, social class, gender, sexual orientation, special needs, and religious diversity (Banks, 2019; T. Howard, 2020). As schools continue to become more diverse in the religious orientation of their students, it will be necessary for educators to have some knowledge of Islam.

Since September 11, 2001, Islam has become labeled in the American media as a religion of terrorists. Unbeknownst to the masses of people, Islam has long existed in the United States, known to the first Africans who were brought to America in 1555 and even studied in secret by several founding fathers (Conyers & Pitre, 2016). Most educators in K-12 schools and professors of teacher-preparation programs are Christian. Teacher-education students in their educator-preparation programs may take multicultural education courses, but these usually do not include a study of Islam.

The Nation of Islam's members are considered unorthodox Muslims. In part, the Nation of Islam's belief that God appeared in person has caused its members to be cast outside mainstream Islam. In addition, the Nation's teaching about race and the origin of Whites has been problematic for many orthodox Muslims.

Several writers try to frame the Nation of Islam as a strange cult or a group of Black radicals who should be ignored and possibly attacked. On the contrary, Elijah Muhammad's teachings were much more detailed than media writers have disclosed. Chapter 4 will discuss the teachings of Elijah Muhammad in more depth. Unlike that of Muslims in the orthodox world, Elijah Muhammad's work in America addressed nearly four hundred years of chattel slavery; thus, his teachings highlighted issues of race and racism.

In his teachings, through historical discourse, he noted the role of Christianity in keeping Blacks in servitude. Unlike civil rights leaders who were protesting injustices and praying to a White Christ figure, Elijah Muhammad sought to disrupt the image of Whites as divine. He was not concerned with integrating into the mainstream society, which he claimed would never give Blacks freedom, justice, and equality.

As a result, he spent his lifetime building a nation within a nation. Moreover, he developed a new culture, one that threw off the alien culture that was a result of slavery and oppression. He was a reformer and life giver to the oppressed, and his teachings were electric, causing a transformation in their lives through the acquisition of knowledge.

While the world marvels at Malcolm X, he was only one of many exceptional students that Elijah Muhammad taught. What Elijah Muhammad offered in the way of education could radically transform the education not only of the oppressed but also of those in the dominant group. An ultimate goal of Islam was to create a universal bond among the whole of humanity.

"Islam"—according to Elijah Muhammad—means "peace," and its adherents are called "Muslim," which means "one who submits their will completely to Allah (God)" (Muhammad, 1965). Elijah Muhammad points out that the name "Allah" is the proper name of God because people use the word "God" casually. And while some opponents of Elijah Muhammad's teachings declare he was not a Muslim because he addressed racism, he was in fact growing his students into a spiritual consciousness while disclosing the origins of White rule in America and throughout the world.

For educators, Islam is strange, and the name "Muhammad" can cause them to view Elijah Muhammad negatively. Those reared in religious settings that depict Jesus and all the prophets as White men see Islam as a heathen religion opposed to Jesus. White supremacist ideology, like the matrix, lies deep beneath the consciousness of some educators, and they are reluctant to learn about anyone who does not have a stamp of approval from those ruling society. Education becomes an opium that deadens consciousness.

Elijah Muhammad's entire mission was the reeducation of Blacks in America. Islam represented the highest form of this education. By degrees, he started reeducating Blacks in America by asking a question raised by curriculum scholars: What knowledge is most important? He taught that the knowledge of God and the knowledge of self were the keys to education (E. Muhammad, 1965).

When he declared that he was taught by God in person for three years and four months, he was placed under surveillance. His first arrest was for refusing to put Muslim children in public schools (E. Muhammad, 1965). Those ruling the society knew that if they controlled the schooling of Muslim children, they would be able to shape their worldview.

For Elijah Muhammad, Islam was the cornerstone of the education process. The Holy Quran was the guiding light that would give Blacks a universal education and raise them to spiritual consciousness. This awakened spiritual consciousness would spark their creative genius, which had been put to sleep through the institution of slavery (E. Muhammad, 1974). They would be required to *read*, as dictated by the first words revealed to the prophet Muhammad:

> *96:1* Read in the name of thy Lord Who creates—
> *96:2* Creates man from a clot,
> *96:3* Read and thy Lord is most Generous,
> *96:4* Who taught by the pen,
> *96:5* Taught man what he knew not (Sura 96: 1–5, Holy Quran)

In reading, they would no longer be an *ummi*, or "unlearned," people. And while many thought his teachings centered only on race, he taught on everything in the universe. With only a fourth-grade education, he declared, "Islam goes as far back as Mathematics. The root of Mathematics goes as far back as Islam" (E. Muhammad, 1965, 1993c). Islam, according to his teaching, is not a religion but a way of life. It is not in contrast to the teachings of Jesus. Islam exposes one to the practices that produced the divine mind in Jesus.

Jesus, a teacher himself, was a threat to the ruling powers because his teachings were making people conscious of how their current way of living enslaved them to a lower form of life. The animalistic behaviors that supported materialism—which resulted in profit for the rich while enslaving the masses—when disclosed by Jesus caused him to be hated. Jesus taught that one should not worry about what one will eat or wear because God provides for his creation and declared the kingdom of God is within you (Luke 17:21 KJV). This aligns with Elijah Muhammad's teaching about the knowledge of self.

For Elijah Muhammad, God was asleep in the Black man; the king of his dome had to be replaced with a new ruler. The teachings of Elijah Muhammad are not antithetical to those of Jesus but are the same. He wrote, "I'll tell you the true meaning of Christian which refers to us the Muslims" (E. Muhammad, 1974, p. 50). Elijah Muhammad was describing what might be considered Chrislam.

Chrislam is a combination of Christianity and Islam, purported to have been founded among the Yoruba of Nigeria (Janson, 2016). However, the unity of Christianity and Islam dates to when Prophet Muhammad's wife Khadija's Christian cousin Waraqa bin Naufal told him that he was the chosen of God after he received his first revelations (Shah, 2014).

It could also be argued that the Nation of Islam is a forerunner of Chrislam. Minister Louis Farrakhan led the Million Man March, most of whose participants were Christian. And he has openly declared, "I am a Muslim—but I am also a Christian and a Jew" (Farrakhan, 2012). It may very well be that a proper understanding of Islam, one that is not told by traditionalists, will lead to a oneness of faith and create relationships that transcend phenotype.

CRITIQUING SOCIAL JUSTICE

The new wave of educational discourse that is centered around social justice needs to be critiqued a bit more. Nieto and Bode (2018) wrote that social justice is a "philosophy, an approach, and actions that embody treating all people with fairness, respect, dignity and generosity" (p. 12). Sleeter and Grant (2009) viewed social justice as way to combat oppression and inequality.

It could be argued that Blacks in America have been the forerunners of social justice discourse ever since they arrived in America on slave ships. Their efforts to escape slavery ranged from committing suicidal acts on the ships that carried them to America to their revolts on the plantations (Hine et al., 2009). There are many unsung Black leaders who emerged to challenge the oppressive living conditions that slavery wrought. In the context of education, critical Black pedagogues are rarely mentioned.

The White educators who support or advocate for social justice are considered the lead torchbearers for educational equality. Thus, Marcus Garvey, Booker T. Washington, Septima Clark, Nannie Helen Burroughs, Carter G. Woodson, and Elijah Muhammad, among many others, are absent from the conversation around what is needed to improve the education of Black students.

One example of this is educator licensure exams, which, while claiming to be a driving force in ensuring teachers are prepared to teach in diverse settings, do not include the philosophical orientations of critical Black educators (Pitre, 2019). Yet educational researchers and politicians purport that something needs to be done to improve the educational outcomes of Black students. However, they do not explore changing the literature that those preparing to become educators should read or be tested on.

Where does Marcus Garvey or Carter G. Woodson factor into the licensure exams for educators? The foundation that undergirds the preparation of teachers and school leaders is premised on literature that will not set those suffering under oppression free. And because those in power can determine the literature that educators read, it is one of the skillful ways they can continue to rule.

Carter G. Woodson (1999) recognized this strategy and called it "miseducation." He argued that under the guise of education, Blacks were internalizing White supremacy. Woodson (1999) wrote that Black educators had been immersed in a Eurocentric education and were figureheads who were following the instructions of their oppressors.

Those shaping society control the literature that teachers and students read, which makes education a political act and has resulted in it being a centerpiece of American political discourse (Spring, 2011). Politicians contend that education is the catalyst of a better economic system (Spring, 2016), and they argue big companies are more likely to reside in communities where educational systems are thriving. Human capitalist ideology, a belief that the goal of schools should be to produce workers, is driving educational policy (Spring, 2011). In the paraphrased words of Elijah Muhammad, the owners of the country need workers.

Elijah Muhammad vehemently argued that the problem was not civil rights per se but that Blacks in America should strive for *human* rights. To effectively argue for human rights, he had to destroy the scientific myths that were used to declare that Whites were the superior people. These scientific myths of White superiority led to laws that supported this belief and cast all other racial groups beyond the human pale, particularly Blacks. Diangelo (2018), in *White Fragility: Why It's So Hard for White People to Talk about Racism*, relayed that of all the groups that Whites despise, Blacks experience the harshest treatment, which she describes as *anti-Black racism*.

In declaring that the White man is the devil, Elijah Muhammad raised a question: How could Whites be like God and treat other human beings with such cruelty and injustice? His goal as the *Messenger of God* was to declare that God had appeared in America to bring freedom, justice, and equality to Blacks and other historically oppressed groups. This meant that Blacks should not be striving to integrate into the dominant Western-centric world but should be trying to separate from it. Paulo Freire (2018) similarly argued that the oppressed are locked inside the structures of the oppressor, which limits their ability to be completely free.

For Elijah Muhammad, the cry was not for social justice but for equal justice. He used historical truths to advocate for equal justice and was seeking complete freedom from White control. In seeking freedom, he articulated historical perspectives that were completely different from what the masses were taught in school. He offered a different world-view for the study of history. Contemporary books like Joel Spring's 2016 *Deculturalization and the Struggle for Equality* and William Watkins's 2001 *The White Architects of Black Education* support Elijah Muhammad's teachings, and these types of readings are rarely required in teacher-preparation programs.

As a result of not gaining a multicultural historical perspective on education, future teachers might enter the profession with deficit thinking. Moreover, it could be argued that the absence of historical literature taught to teacher-education candidates means they are not provided an African-centered historical overview of Black history that predates the American experience (Asante, 2005).

For example, social foundations textbooks scantly cover the educational history of Blacks in America. Furthermore, they do not provide a detailed history of Blacks that dates to ancient civilizations. Maulana Karenga's (2002) textbook *An Introduction to Black Studies*, which includes a chapter about great African civilizations, would not be studied by educators. As a result, many educators believe that civilization began with Europeans.

This historical misinformation has led to White supremacist ideology, and Elijah Muhammad disrupted this thinking when he declared that the original man was the Asiatic Black man. Crushing Eurocentric perspectives, he taught that the history of Blacks dates to God's self-creation over sixty-six trillion years ago:

> How came the Black God, Mr. Muhammad? He is self-created. How could self create self? Take your magnifying glass and start looking at these little atoms out here in front of you. You see they are egged shaped and they are oblong. You can crack them open and you will find everything in them that you find out here. . . . Imagine, you close your eyes

now; imagine the whole entire visibility of the Universe is gone from you. This is the way he was born: in total darkness. (E. Muhammad, 1974, p. 39)

In the word "atom," you get the enunciation of the word "Adam," the first human in the creation story. In the ancient history of African religion is the Dogon's origin of creation regarding the egg, and it is similar to the teachings of Elijah Muhammad (Karenga, 2002). The fact that African civilizations predate White existence is problematic because it disrupts White supremacy (Asante, 2017).

In *Revolutionary Pedagogy*, Molefi Asante (2017) points out that classical African civilizations are not included in the educational discourse. The African origins of human civilization caused Elijah Muhammad to ask how Whites could be superior if, in their travels, they found the Black man's imprints in these lands prior to their arrival (E. Muhammad, 1967). These critiques and disclosures made Elijah Muhammad hated. He did not view justice as inclusion but saw it as being empowered to discover one's self.

The clamor around social justice in many ways is what Paulo Freire (2018) referred to as "false generosity," which will not lead to complete freedom. Social justice is like a fad that does not seek to create a new order but rather, through skillful language, like "inclusion," does not shift the power dynamics. Those from historically oppressed groups should ask whose systems and structures are being included. Asante argued that the term "inclusion" suggests that those in power are still making the ground rules (Conyers, 2017). Elijah Muhammad (1965, 1965) was aware of this inclusionary discourse and argued that it was a *trick* designed by those governing the society to take Black people with them to their doom.

The study of Elijah Muhammad's teachings is threatening to a wide range of leaders because it has the potential to help Blacks discover their uniqueness. For the most part, educators, no matter how radical they are perceived to be, do not possess a body of knowledge that will produce *gods*. This was the goal of Elijah Muhammad's reeducation program, and he openly said to Blacks, "He sent me to tell you these things to make gods out of you" (Muhammad, 2006, p. 80).

This type of teaching is unheard of to educators because they have been trained to view education as the pathway to a job. Their role as educators is not a spiritual undertaking; it's about preparing students to pass an end-of-year exam. Even the brightest professors of education would be disturbed to hear education should make Blacks in America into gods. For teacher-education professors, a study of Elijah Muhammad's most notable student, Louis Farrakhan, is problematic because of the powerful ruling forces that have muddied his image.

In addition, he espouses bodies of knowledge that can usher in a new educational paradigm, one that is outside the scope of the Eurocentric canon (Pitre, 2018). Farrakhan's critiques of Whiteness are described as hate teachings. These critiques have caused the media to portray him in the most negative light, and he is the litmus test for Blacks aspiring to greatness in the White-dominant world. Derrick Bell (1992), the father of critical race theory, praised Minister Farrakhan in *Faces at the Bottom of the Well*. In the book, he describes Minister Farrakhan as bright and super articulate. Despite his praise for Farrakhan, educational scholars have not mentioned Farrakhan in their writings.

Farrakhan, like his teacher, is the embodiment of knowledge. Through the dissemination of knowledge, he has influenced people across the globe, causing him to be a national security threat. Blacks can play sports and sing songs, but they should never have a knowledge surpassing that of those ruling society.

CONCLUSION

Most writings about Elijah Muhammad and the Nation of Islam paint a negative picture of the group—from Beynon's labeling the Nation of Islam as a "voodoo cult" back in 1938 to other writings that have been part of the FBI's propaganda campaign to stop the Nation's growth. Many of the studies about Elijah Muhammad do not disclose how the authors established credibility and trustworthiness.

For the most part, they were written to slander or profit through gossip and innuendo under the guise of providing new information. One example is Edward Montgomery's 1963 *Los Angeles Herald Examiner* article titled "Black Muslim Founder Exposed as White." Montgomery has been described as a water boy for the FBI with a history of writing false articles (Kamiya, 2017). He became one of the first journalists who practiced yellow journalism, which is the writing of articles that are untrue but sensationalized to get an audience.

To date, these false narratives are carried in books such as *The Dead Are Rising: The Life of Malcolm X*, where they provide inaccurate details regarding the establishment of the Nation of Islam (Payne & Payne, 2021). Elijah Muhammad understood the propaganda of lies that would be spewed against him by his study of history, causing him to say, "All messengers, prophets, or apostles of the past, we find that people always did not believe in them and considered them to be liars" (N. Hakim, 1997, p. 65).

The purported major books on the Nation of Islam and Elijah Muhammad are published by companies whose owners are in opposition to their teachings. Thus, they get the best editors who can skillfully use language that mixes truth with falsehood to intentionally disparage Elijah Muhammad.

The best sources for studying Elijah Muhammad are his books and speeches. Through a collection of this material, along with queries to students of these teachings, researchers would have a more balanced perspective. The knowledge that Elijah Muhammad disclosed could not have been known by a person with a fourth-grade education coming out of slavery. In fact, what he taught is not known to most people who have graduated with doctoral degrees from the best colleges and universities.

Sadly, his teachings have not been disclosed to the masses, who, through propaganda, have been tricked to stay away from his teachings, although those ruling society have used these teachings to fuel many of their modern advancements. The field of education, a traditionally conservative field despite its growing focus on social justice, continues to relegate critical Black pedagogues to a sidebar in the educational discourse. Moreover, after 9/11, the fear of Islam has caused the masses of people to have a negative view of the faith. The religiosity of educators limits their interest in studying the teachings of Elijah Muhammad. Many teachers see Islam as an anti-Christ religion that is against the teachings of Jesus.

Elijah Muhammad had to bear many insults, lies, and innuendos for his *teachings*, but he had a belief that Islam, like the sun, in its due time would eventually dispel the falsehoods that kept people from seeing the beauty of God's creation that was sleeping inside of them. Proper education rooted in the knowledge of self would help human beings be *born again* through the renewing of their minds.

In part, his contributions have caused a groundswell of knowledge that is now emerging in diverse fields of study. In his 1974 book *Our Savior Has Arrived*, Muhammad talks in Chapter 23 ("He Makes All Things New") about new fuels that would be used in automobiles that would not pollute the air. Today there are electric cars, and the goal is to move away from traditional fuels such as gas and oil. The new cars, with their artificial intelligence, were discussed in Elijah Muhammad's discourse on the Mother Wheel. The fields of education, social justice, critical pedagogy, and multicultural education all have tenets that are similar to Elijah Muhammad's teachings.

The growing diversity in America's public schools has led to discourse around preparing educators for diverse student populations (Banks, 2019; Esmail et al., 2017). Included in the multicultural education discourse are critical theories that mirror Elijah Muhammad's teachings (Apple, 2019; Esmail & Pitre, 2018; Ladson-Billings & Tate, 1995; McLaren, 2015). One area under the multicultural education umbrella is an examination of religious diversity in schools. While several universities offer courses and degrees in the preparation of educators, Islam does not factor into the conversation.

In part, Islam provides an education that touches every discipline of study, making it a liberating force that does not require a monetary fee. It's free, and many believe it is freeing to the human soul. Its primary text—the Holy Quran—is a scientific book that compels its adherents to *do good*. As a reformer and life giver, Elijah Muhammad had to breathe knowledge into the dry bones that had suffered not only physical death but also spiritual death. His major task was teaching!

He brought a *light* that is fueling many of the scientific and technological advances that we are currently experiencing and has the keys to a body of knowledge that will unlock the enslaved mind to produce a new human being. Elijah Muhammad's entire mission was education, and his teachings continue to be a threat to those in exceedingly high places.

Chapter Three

Humble Beginnings

Scholars and practitioners in the field of education are faced with the challenge of educating diverse student populations. They have explored numerous innovations in an effort to improve the educational plight of diverse students. There is widespread discourse in the United States about closing the achievement gap (Ladson-Billings, cited in Pitre, 2021a; T. Howard, 2020). In schools across America and even abroad, students are languishing in prison-like structures that never allow them to discover their true selves.

Black students bear the brunt of high-stakes testing, which is a throwback to the eugenics movement that gave birth to intelligence tests, which support racism and White supremacy (Hilliard, 1995; Watkins, 2001). Under the guise of equity, policymakers have weaponized education against Black and other historically underserved students (Pitre & Hudson, 2020). Carter G. Woodson (1999) described weaponized education in the following way: "As another has well said, to handicap a student by teaching him that his black face is a curse and that his struggle to change his condition is hopeless is the worst sort of lynching" (p. 24).

In nearly every negative category, Blacks are overrepresented; most schools that are considered failing are majority Black and Hispanic (T. Howard, 2020). This is coupled with the fact that teacher-education programs are primarily framed from a Eurocentric lens. In addition, several of these teacher-education programs may not address deficit thinking, racism, or teacher incongruence (Pitre et al., 2021).

Sleeter (2004) wrote, "A predominantly white teaching force in a rac-ist and multicultural society is not good for anyone" (p. 163). Moreover, teacher-education professors are faced with the challenge of working in a field that is forcing many of them to become more like test-prepara-tion coordinators (Kohli, 2009). Additionally, non-White professors in teacher-education programs may experience racism from colleagues, administrators, and students (Ladson-Billings, 2005). If there is a real concern about improving the educational experiences of Black and other historically underserved students, there is a need to look beyond the traditional philosophies and methods.

This chapter begins by providing a historical overview of the Black experience in America through the lens of Elijah Muhammad's teach-ings. It then provides a brief biographical section that focuses par-ticularly on Elijah Muhammad's life experiences in Georgia, where he witnessed two lynchings, and discusses his journey into the Nation of Islam.

The biographical section includes information that comes directly from the words of Elijah Muhammad. This is purposely done to allow his voice to be heard because most of the research studies about him have been written to keep the masses away from his teachings. Smith (2012) cogently captured the way researchers have reported their find-ings about groups like the Nation of Islam when he noted that many of these researchers have been rewarded for disclosing lies and half-truths.

For the most part, research studies about the Nation of Islam have provided false narratives about the group because many of them were part of the counterintelligence program seeking to destroy Black orga-nizations that awakened the consciousness of Blacks. Because Elijah Muhammad articulated a message to Blacks in America that raised them to new levels of consciousness, he became an enemy of the state. Moreover, he attacked the theological underpinnings that fueled White supremacy, declaring that the origin of all life began with a Black God who gave birth to an entire universe.

THE IMPORTANCE OF HISTORY

Elijah Muhammad (1965) taught that of all studies that one could undertake, the study of history is best suited to reward the researcher.

Educator-preparation programs do not address the history of Blacks in America that predates their enslavement in America. And even when teacher-education students have opportunities to read a few lines related to Black history, they are often not taught from an African-centered perspective; nor do they learn how to apply this knowledge in an educational setting.

An African-centered approach means viewing the world from the perspective of Africans and African Americans (Asante, 1991). An African-centered approach, when applied to the study of history, can be helpful in disrupting long-standing racial and social inequalities. The lies that teachers have been told throughout their years of schooling promote racism (Lowen, 2007). For example, prior to the 1960s, most history courses glamorized a group of White men called the "founding fathers," despite the fact they saw Blacks as three-fifths of a human being.

These *founding fathers* believed their race and wealth made them better than others, which in turn allowed them to fashion laws that disregarded the humanity of those who were not of their race or social class. Frederick Douglass captures this duality of being American in his speech "What to the Slave Is the Fourth of July" (Pitre, 2019).

Douglass highlighted that while Whites were basking in the greatness of independence, it was sham and disgrace to Blacks in America (Pitre, 2019). His critique of the nation's celebration of its freedom from Great Britain formed the foundation for an African-centered approach to viewing history. Likewise, Elijah Muhammad went into detail about the origin of the "Black man," and he articulated a knowledge that shattered the foundation upon which White rule was premised.

Regarding the early history of Blacks in America, Elijah Muhammad taught that the first Blacks came to America in 1555 on a slave ship called *Jesus*. They were tricked by John Hawkins, who promised that they would find gold and luxuries in the New World. Once they arrived in the new land, the promise of gold and luxury never materialized, causing the newly arrived people to realize they had been tricked.

Most history books say the first Blacks arrived in Jamestown in 1619. However, Elijah Muhammad taught that a sixty-four-year period is left out of the history books. This sixty-four-year history was so brutal and diabolical that it was not disclosed to the masses, and it is often referred to as the $64,000 question.

These sixty-four years included a breaking process where Blacks were stripped of their names, languages, and cultures. It was the original brainwashing that was designed to erase Blacks' historical memory of their native land. The first Blacks who arrived in America were not slaves but had been put through a process that would make a slave—*brain washing*.

Babies were taken from their mothers and were not taught their native language. Newly arrived Blacks were put through a breaking process that made them Negroes. *Negro*, when the *c* is genuflected, becomes *Necro*, which means "dead" (Akbar, 1998). A once-living people were now dead to their former selves and had become *real estate*. As real estate, they were property, and every attempt was made to keep them in a state of servitude.

Malcolm X declared that Blacks were scientifically made by the "white man":

> But once our names were taken and our language was taken and our identity was destroyed and our roots cut off with no history, we became like a stump, something dead, a twig over here in the Western Hemisphere. Anybody could step on us, trample us, or burn us, and there would be nothing we could do about it. (Pitre, 2019, p. 63)

This process rendered Black people mentally dead, and it was the reason that Elijah Muhammad declared that his mission was the resurrection of the dead, meaning that Blacks in America had been placed in this condition by those owning the country, whom he described as the *slave masters*.

When the Constitution was framed, it was written in the interest of property-owning White men. Leaders like George Washington and Thomas Jefferson were slaveholders. Not only were Blacks impacted, but also Native Americans were virtually extinguished. Their land was stolen, and as part of the "education" process, their children were placed in boarding schools (Spring, 2016).

The motto for educating Native Americans was premised on taking away their culture and making them see the world through a European lens. The *apple* represented White educational dominance because it allowed natives to keep their outer physical appearance while simultaneously having a White worldview.

The Hispanic populations received similar treatment, as they were removed from their lands in the western United States. They faced hostile educational policies that sought to remove their native languages and were forced to speak English. In addition, White supremacist attitudes caused entire Hispanic communities to be uprooted out of places like southeastern Texas. Spring (2016) wrote,

> Frederick Law Olmsted recorded many of these attitudes while traveling through Texas in 1855 and 1856 as a reporter for the *New York Times*. Olmsted overheard newly arrived settlers complaining that Mexican Americans "think themselves as good as white men" and they were "vermin to be exterminated." (p. 94)

The colonialists held White supremacist attitudes toward all the aboriginal peoples they encountered. European colonialists forced Native Americans and Hispanics from their lands and placed them in schools that were designed to make them view the world from their oppressor's perspective.

When Abraham Lincoln signed the Emancipation Proclamation, the newly freed Blacks had been completely cut off from their ancestral roots for a little over three hundred years. Blacks were now speaking English despite the fact that they were not from England. Their names were taken and replaced with the names of their slave owners. This caused Malcolm X to ask Black people, "What was your name? It couldn't have been Bush or Jones" (Dhaliwal, 2015). Malcolm's critique made Blacks conscious that they were still the property of Whites because they maintained their slave masters' names.

He was reiterating the words of his teacher, Elijah Muhammad (1965), who said, "How can the so-called Negro say that his name is Sam Jones, a white man's name with roots in Europe, when Sam Jones (Black Man) comes from Africa or Asia" (p. 54). Moreover, during slavery, it was a crime for Blacks to learn to read. Reading was threatening to the slave owners because it could potentially stimulate resistance. If Blacks were caught reading, this could lead to a severe beating or death (Spring, 2016).

The aristocratic class of America is linked to Blacks, and there are untold stories of Blaxploitation. The use of Black female bodies for the pleasure of White slave owners has been well documented. Even Thomas Jefferson's fathering of children with his slave Sarah

Hemmings has been discussed, but there is very little discussion of Black male bodies being used for the pleasure of White rulers (Foster, 2011).

Lincoln's Emancipation Proclamation would not free Blacks from the psychological chains of nearly four hundred years of slavery or from the control of those governing society (Akbar, 1998). After the Civil War, in 1865, a group of wealthy White men met to chart an educational plan for the newly freed Blacks and people living in the South (Watkins, 2001).

They crafted a seventy-five-year educational plan with the intent of making Blacks docile and amenable to White rule (Watkins, 2001). In the education of Blacks, Christianity was one tool used to support White supremacist ideology. Gary Howard (2006), in *We Can't Teach What We Don't Know: White Teachers in Multiracial Schools*, captured how Christianity was used to colonize aboriginal people, writing, "In addition to the devastating loss of life and land, the use of the Bible and Christianity as tools of oppression has been a particularly sad chapter in the establishment of White dominance" (p. 40).

While Whites sought to use the Bible as a tool to make Blacks subservient to White rule, Blacks like Denmark Vessey and Gabriel Prossey used it to justify their fight for freedom. Elijah Muhammad also used the Bible as the primary text to liberate Blacks in America.

The early of education of Blacks was premised on a European construction of Christianity. These White architects of Black education presented images and narratives that supported White supremacy. At the very root of Black education is a religious orientation that supported the interests of those ruling society.

For his critique of the White majoritarian narrative of Christianity, Elijah Muhammad became a heretic because he taught historical truths that exposed the ideology that gave birth to structural racism and inequality. When he critiqued Christianity as a slave-making religion, this caused him to become disliked by not only Whites but also Blacks, who had been educated through a hidden curriculum to believe Whites were the superior people. The hidden curriculum is not part of the formal curriculum but is internalized by students.

Jesus and the disciples were all White men, giving credence to why White, property-owning men ruled society. The names in the Bible, like David and Paul, were English names even though these people lived in the Middle East or Africa, where those names did not exist. The

Western construction of Christianity was like a hidden curriculum that lay beneath the consciousness. Civil rights leaders could protest for the right to ride at the front of a bus but would pray to a White Jesus for justice. Frances Welsing (1991) wrote that these experiences produced in the masses a belief that Whites are superior:

> Thus all Black and other non-white peoples who profess to be members of the Christian (white supremacy) religion, whether they are conscious or not, worship the white man as God (not as a god, but as "the" God) . . . the Being perfect in power, wisdom and goodness whom men worship as creator and ruler of the universe. (p. 168)

Once Blacks were placed in schools, the White architects of education constructed a curriculum that was premised on White supremacy. The curriculum focused on characters such as the founding fathers, and the stories that were told to children in the early grades depicted all White images. Moreover, knowledge was constructed in a way to glamorize Whiteness. A good example of this is the narrative around Malcolm X.

The majoritarian narrative purports Malcolm went to Mecca and had an epiphany that resulted in him believing that Whites were no longer bad. They then pit Malcolm against Elijah Muhammad, declaring that after his visit to Mecca, he threw off these racist teachings and became more mainstream. The Reverend Dr. Martin Luther King Jr. was championed because he had a dream that all people could get along. They never mention Dr. King's meeting with Elijah Muhammad and its impact on his worldview. Nieto and Bode (2018) pointed out that the only time non-Whites are highlighted in textbooks used in schools is when they fit into the dominant narrative.

The education of Blacks in America is a major concern for those ruling society. For many years, they have sought to control the light (knowledge) that could come to Blacks in America. This prompted Elijah Muhammad (1965) to discuss through historical record what one of the congressmen said regarding the education of Blacks in the South: "We have as far as possible closed every avenue by which light may enter the slave's mind" (p. 186).

The light represents knowledge, and this quote outlines how those ruling society were intentional about controlling what Black people learned. Critical theorists in education like Michael Apple (2019) have described this as the selective tradition, which means that those in power determine what knowledge is used in schools. Throughout America's history, those in the ruling group have shaped educational systems to gain access to a labor supply while never truly empowering the masses to maximize their human potential.

These architects of Black education spent more money on crafting an educational agenda for Blacks than the government did (Gatto, 2017; Watkins, 2001). Today the superrich contribute millions of dollars to influence educational policy. Spring (2011) wrote about the powerful influence that think tanks and foundations play in shaping educational policy.

Woodson's (1999) argument that the education of Black people was entirely in the hands of those who enslaved and oppressed them still rings true. Elijah Muhammad would echo this by saying, "Our former slave-masters, knowing of our dependence upon them, maliciously and gratefully adopted attitudes and social and educational systems that have deprived us of the opportunity to become free and independent right up to the present day" (p. 227).

Education and the process of educating are divine acts. Every prophet that appeared brought a knowledge or a literature to the people to whom they were sent. According to Elijah Muhammad, the great secret in America was the lost tribe or people who were buried in the West.

Under symbolism, the plight of Blacks in America was described in scriptures and other books. For example, Elijah Muhammad taught that when the Bible says, "For as lightning that comes from the east is visible even in the west, so will be the coming of the Son of Man" (Matthew 24:27 NIV), it is referring to the coming of God to America to bring justice to the Blacks who experienced slavery, suffering, and death.

He taught that God had visited America, fulfilling what was written in the book of Genesis, which states, "Know for certain that for four hundred years your descendants will be strangers in a country not their own and that they will be enslaved and mistreated there. But I will punish the nation they serve as slaves, and afterward they will come out with great possessions" (Genesis 15:13–14 NIV).

When policymakers crafted the separation of church and state, this paved the way to ensure public schools would provide an official knowledge that keeps the masses away from the great secret of God's appearance to free those suffering under oppressive White rule. If the Supreme Being is expected to come, it would be wise to not mention this in the education discourse; therefore, Elijah Muhammad is not included because he believed education begins with the question Who is God?

LIFE ON A CROSS

For over forty years Elijah Muhammad suffered extreme persecution because he sought to deliver a message to Blacks in America. It was a message that he believed would free Blacks from the oppressive conditions brought on by their enslavement. From his early childhood experiences to his leadership of the Nation of Islam, he endured a lifetime of suffering. A careful reading of various biographies highlights the numerous *cross* experiences he encountered (Clegg, 1997; Halasa, 1990; N. Hakim, 1997; Sahib, 1951).

The exact date of Elijah Muhammad's birth is not certain, but he selected October 7, 1897. He was one of thirteen children born to William and Mariah Poole. Prior to his birth, his mother had visions that she would one day give birth to a child who would change the course of human affairs (Clegg, 1997). As a child he exhibited leadership skills by resolving conflicts between his siblings (Clegg, 1997).

His father William was a Baptist preacher in the area and a sharecropper. As a little boy, he was afforded the opportunity to sit in the area where the preachers would sit. Pampered in this setting, he began to have aspirations of one day becoming a preacher. His interest in preaching inspired him to read the Bible so much that he was teasingly called Elijah, the prophet.

Born only thirty-two years after the Civil War, he was forced to leave school in the fourth grade to help his family with maintaining the necessities of life. He and his sister would cut wood together, which would later be sold in nearby Cordele, Georgia (Sahib, 1951). At the age of ten, he witnessed a lynching in the town square:

> Once, a time when I was a little boy coming to Cordele to sell a load of wood, I saw a lynching crowd. I was that time a child about ten years old, when I saw that morning a dark man lynched by whites. . . . They took him and hanged him on a willow tree after they had lynched him with extreme cruelty. (Sahib, 1951, p. 19)

This horrible experience would haunt him for the rest of his life, causing him to say, "That event impressed me so much that I cannot get
over it; I did never forget it; not until this day" (Sahib, 1951, p. 19). On
another occasion, at the age of twenty-three, he observed another lynching where a Black man had been dragged through the streets by a truck.

When he moved to Detroit, Michigan, he observed two Black men
killed on the streets (Sahib, 1951). He would later say that in the rural
South, they lynch Blacks on trees, but in the North, they shoot them in
the street without justice. The events around the 2020 killing of George
Floyd and others by policemen were all familiar to Elijah Muhammad.

In 1917, he met Clara Evans at a church function. They began dating despite the disapproval of Clara's father. Clara's father didn't want
her dating Elijah because he was too poor to support her as a husband.
Despite Quartus Evans's disapproval, the couple eloped on March 17,
1919 (Z. Muhammad, 2020). To support his family, Elijah worked for
White men.

On one occasion, while working for a White employer, he observed
him calling Black people outside their names. In addition, this White
employer had his wife whip Black employees if they did not satisfy his
work demands (Sahib, 1951). This White employer had given Elijah the
nickname "Levy" and threatened to whip him like he had done other
Black employees.

Elijah told his White employer that he would retaliate if the man
tried to physically assault him. Having experienced the lynching of
Black men and the deeply entrenched racism of the South, he decided
to move his wife and two small children to Detroit, Michigan (Sahib,
1951). Regarding his move, he said, "I was in born in Georgia, and was
never out of the state of Georgia, until I was 25 years of age. I married
and had two children and moved to Detroit in April 1923 from Macon
Georgia" (N. Hakim, 1997, p. 35).

His parents had already left Georgia and were living in Detroit. He
found Detroit to be similar to Georgia with regard to the oppression that
Blacks experienced. He said of his experience in Detroit, "I moved to
Detroit because I thought life might be better, but even there the first
year I saw my people shot down right on the street without any justice
whatsoever" (Sahib, 1951, p. 67). Unable to find work, he began to
drink heavily, and his wife would find him in the alley too drunk to find
his way home (Taylor, 2017).

In extremely poor living conditions, his father had a conversation with him about one of his friends who had joined the Nation of Islam. His father's friend had changed his name to Abdul Muhammad and related to him some of the teachings of a person named Mr. Fard (Sahib, 1951). At first, Elijah was reluctant to hear about Islam because, like most, he saw it as a pagan religion (J. Muhammad, 1996). Despite this, he and his brother decided to visit with Abdul Muhammad. During these visits, he became impressed and wanted to hear Mr. Fard.

He attempted to hear a lecture on more than one occasion but missed seeing Mr. Fard. On another occasion, it was too crowded, and as a result he had to listen from a distance. Finally, on August 22, 1931, he was able to take in a lecture (J. Muhammad, 1996). After the lecture, all listeners could shake Mr. Fard's hand. Elijah approached Mr. Fard and whispered into his ear that he knew who he was: the long-awaited messiah, Jesus, whom the world had been expecting to come for the last two thousand years (N. Hakim, 1997).

Fard whispered back, "Yes, I am the One, but who knows that except yourself? Be quiet" (N. Hakim 1997, p. 39). At a later time, when Elijah asked him, "Who are you and what is your real name?" he replied, "I am the one that the world has been expecting for the past 2000 years" (E. Muhammad, 1965, p. 16). To this response, Elijah queried, "What is your real name?" And his response was, "My name is Mahdi; I am God, I came to guide you into the right path that you may be successful and see the hereafter" (E. Muhammad, 1965, p. 16).

He went on to describe the destruction of the present world through bombs and poison gas. He then showed Elijah a destructive-looking plane that he called the Mother of Planes, which was a half mile by a half mile and the largest man-made object in the sky during that time (E. Muhammad, 1965).

In popular culture, the movie *Independence Day* has many similarities to what Elijah Muhammad described about the Mother of Planes. Additionally, Elijah Muhammad's teachings about the Mother of Planes discussed artificial intelligence. Today the citing of UFOs is common, and government officials in various countries have acknowledged the existence of these objects (R. Muhammad, 2013).

Wallace D. Fard's birth on February 26, 1877, according to Elijah Muhammad, was in fulfillment of the second coming of Jesus. Mr. Fard's father was in the circle of men who hold the secret knowledge of the universe (E. Muhammad, 1993c). They are described in the Bible as the twenty-four elders. Elijah Muhammad taught that they are divided into twelve major scientists and twelve minor scientists. The twelve major scientists are called the rulers, which explains why there are twelve inches on a ruler (N. Hakim, 1997).

Twelve of these leaders of Islam conferred about the lost tribe, which were the Blacks in America who had been stolen from their homeland and were without the knowledge of themselves (E. Muhammad, 1993c). However, it was predicted by the prophets that there would be a lost tribe at the time of the Judgment.

The council of leaders decided that in order to reach Blacks in America, a messenger would have to be raised from among them. Prior to raising a messenger, someone would have to be prepared to bring knowledge to Blacks in America that would restore them to their original selves, which they had lost because of their enslavement in America. Once prepared for this mission, they would *raise* or *teach* one of the former slaves in America, thus making them a messenger.

Mr. Fard's father realized that he could not get among the people of America because of his dark complexion. As a result, he went into the Caucasus Mountains, where he married a White woman who had been purified of the evil tendencies in her nature. Their first child was a girl, and Mr. Fard was the second child (N. Hakim, 1997). Elijah taught that Fard had been coming in and out of the United States for twenty years before making himself known and had studied every educational system in the civilized world.

The declaration "he studied every educational system of the civilized world" (N. Hakim, 1997, p. 41) makes it definitive that Elijah Muhammad's mission was educational. In addition, in his interview with Sahib (1951), Elijah Muhammad reported the following:

> Mr. Fard told me out of his own mouth that he had been educated in the University of California for twenty years just to prepare himself and be well equipped to save our people. He told me that he was working for this purpose for forty-two years, twenty of them he worked among dark people before he made himself known. (p. 55)

Sahib (1951) reported that this California university that Mr. Fard attended was the University of Southern California; he wrote, "The current Apostle, his wife, and some of the earliest followers in Chicago say that W. D. Fard received his education from the University of Southern California in Los Angeles" (p. 55).

A historical review of major highlights at the University of Southern California (n.d.) shows there was a 1922 conference called the Pan American Conference on Education. In addition, there were seven hundred international students at the University of Southern California, and it was the first university in the country to establish an international studies program.

The international studies program was designed to produce diplomats and educators. Sahib (1951) noted that Fard was initially being prepared for a diplomatic career but abandoned it to bring freedom, justice, and equality to Blacks in America. Tynnetta Muhammad (2021) also notes that Fard Muhammad visited the University of California, Los Angeles, and that he was on the Hollywood scene. Moreover, Elijah Muhammad taught that it would be through the medium of film that people would be informed of future world events (T. Muhammad, 2021).

Fard was no longer underground once he established the Nation of Islam in Detroit. Detroit was a haven for Blacks seeking respite from the economic and racial inequality of the South. The area known as Paradise Valley became the launching pad for Mr. Fard to gain a sizable following. He began by gaining access to the homes of Black Detroiters by acting as a person selling items from the motherland (Beynon, 1938).

Once among them, he would begin teaching deep historical truths. These early listeners began to invite friends over until eventually they had outgrown these homes. They then rented a hall, and the number of listeners began to swell. Fard declared July 4, 1930, as Independence Day for Blacks in America, making it the official birth date of the Nation of Islam (Muhammad, 1974).

The meeting between Mr. Fard and Elijah (Poole) was the beginning of a birthing process that would take the fourth-grade sharecropper's son from the bowels of American society to the pinnacle of leadership. For three years and four months, Fard deposited in Elijah Poole knowledge about everything in the universe (E. Muhammad, 1974). This knowledge would make him a *Messenger* to the Lost Found Blacks in America.

Examples of the knowledge he received ranged from a discussion about life on Mars to many of the popular culture topics around the transcendence of consciousness to neuroethology, futuristic automobiles, sun storms, chemical bacteriologists, and a long list of other advanced scientific teaching. Elijah Muhammad's greatness was in both the teachings that he received from Mr. Fard and his leadership acumen.

Unlike the civil rights leaders of the 1960s, Elijah Muhammad had a knowledge that shook up White rule throughout the planet. After studying under Mr. Fard, he was given the name Abdul Karriem but didn't like it because it was similar to Abdul Muhammad. Abdul Muhammad was a onetime minister in the Nation of Islam who broke from Mr. Fard to set up a splinter group.

Fard then agreed and gave Elijah the last name Muhammad. He disclosed to Elijah that his full name was Wallace D. Fard Muhammad. For his teachings, Fard was arrested and sent for Elijah to visit him. He wanted Elijah to see firsthand some of the suffering he would have to experience in his mission to educate Blacks in America.

During his imprisonment, Fard told police officials more about his identity than he did the Blacks he was teaching. Fard left Detroit and went to Chicago, where he was immediately detained. Ordered not return to Detroit, it is said, he departed to the tears and sorrow of his followers. After Fard's departure, Elijah began to declare that this stranger was God in person. He began to call him *Master Fard Muhammad*.

Like the youth of today, Elijah Muhammad was unconscious of the supreme force in the universe. Found in a drunken state and impoverished when he first met Master Fard Muhammad, his life was completely changed (J. Muhammad, 1996). By the time Master Fard Muhammad departed, he had placed his entire being into the little Black man from Georgia.

Unlike at their first meeting on September 22, 1931, when he whispered into Master Fard Muhammad's ear, "I know who you are," and was told to be quiet and not share this information until after Fard's departure, Elijah Muhammad began to declare that he had met God and that he appeared in the person of Master Fard Muhammad. His words were consistent with the language found in the book of Exodus, where Moses declared God appeared. Even in today's popular culture movies like *Evan Almighty*, the verbiage "God appeared" is used.

Prior to Master Fard Muhammad's departure, he asked the ministers in the Nation of Islam to select whom they thought to be their top minister (Taylor, 2017). After their selection, Master Fard Muhammad declared that his *minister* was Elijah Muhammad. This would later cause jealousy among the group.

After Fard's departure, Elijah Muhammad became the target of others in the movement who thought he should not be the leader (N. Hakim, 1997). When Master Fard Muhammad departed, he had placed the job of *Messenger* on Elijah Muhammad, and this caused jealousy among the members. It was so extreme that even members of his immediate family tried to take his life.

His brother Kalot became one of his main adversaries. As a result of the internal schisms, membership in the Nation of Islam started to dwindle. Elijah Muhammad noted that a majority of its members had become hypocrites (Sahib, 1951).

To avert the loss of life, Elijah Muhammad fled to the East Coast, where he lived with several families under bogus names. While living with these families, he was also spreading the teachings he received from W. D. Fard (N. Hakim, 1997). This led to the spread of Islam on the East Coast.

In an interview with Sahib (1951), he reported that Master Fard Muhammad gave Elijah Muhammad a list of 150 books that he should read. According to Tynnetta Muhammad (2021b), the number of books was 104, and Elijah Muhammad also confirmed this number. While in Washington, DC, he came to the realization that these books were in the Library of Congress. While studying there, he found a picture of himself in one of the books, which would cause him to say that if one were to study, they could find a picture of themselves in a book (J. Muhammad, 1996).

In 1942, while in Washington, DC, Elijah Muhammad was arrested on draft-evasion charges. At the time of his arrest, he pointed out that he was past the age requirement for the draft. Speaking on the reason for his arrest, he said, "In 1943, I was sent to the Federal Penitentiary in Milan, Michigan, for nothing other than to be kept out of the public and from teaching my people the truth during the war between America, Germany, and Japan" (E. Muhammad, 1965, p. 321). Not only was Elijah Muhammad arrested, but also several of his ministers were imprisoned for refusing to participate in the war.

When arrested, he was questioned for several hours. In part, the interrogations were a form of torture designed to mentally break him. In addition, the prison warden did not make accommodations for the

Muslim diet. They attempted to starve the Muslims, and they also deprived them of access to the Holy Quran.

During his prison sentence, it is believed that he contracted bronchitis (Clegg, 1997). This illness would plague him until his death in 1975. The prison experience, which lasted four to five years, caused him to be separated from his wife and children. During his time in prison, Clara Muhammad kept the Nation of Islam afloat by providing correspondence between Elijah and the believers. She also brought typed copies of the Holy Quran for her husband to read while he was in prison because he was not allowed to read it (Z. Muhammad, 2020).

Prior to his arrest, he spent seven years away from his family running from those seeking his life. And his first arrest was in 1934 because he refused to send Muslim children to the Detroit public school (E. Muhammad, 1965). From 1934 to 1946, he suffered the death traps of those who had abandoned the teachings of Mr. Fard as well as the persecution of the US government. In 1946, he was released from prison, but his four-year stay was not in vain because this laid the foundation to recruit future prisoners to Islam. It paved the way for the conversion of Malcolm Little.

When Malcolm Little was arrested in 1946, he was among the many prisoners who were introduced to the teachings of Elijah Muhammad. For Malcolm, the teachings were more personal because his brother was a member of the Nation of Islam. In 1952, when Malcolm was released from prison, he was prepared to assume a role in the Nation of Islam.

With only an eighth-grade education, he was appointed by Elijah Muhammad as the minister of Mosque Number 7 in Harlem, New York, in June 1954 and then made the national spokesman for the Nation of Islam in 1963 (Clegg, 1997). On December 2, 1963, Malcolm was suspended for ninety days for a breach in protocol whereby all members of the Nation of Islam were not to make any comments about the assassination of John Kennedy (Clegg, 1997).

Malcolm, speaking in place of Elijah Muhammad at an event in New York City, delivered a speech titled "God's Judgment on White America." When asked by a reporter about President Kennedy's assassination, he responded that it was a case of chickens coming home to roost (Clegg, 1997).

Malcolm's ninety-day suspension opened the door for agents provocateurs to create a rift between him and Elijah Muhammad (D.

Muhammad, 2020). During the ninety-day silence, tensions developed between the two men. According to Demetric Muhammad (2020), these tensions were fueled by agents provocateurs inside the Nation of Islam. Besides, it was the goal of J. Edgar Hoover and his counterintelligence program to destroy the Nation of Islam. Elijah Muhammad's home in Chicago had been wiretapped since 1957 (Gardell, 1996). He was the most spied-on of all the Black leaders.

The rift between Malcolm X and Elijah Muhammad became more pronounced when Malcolm was asked to move out of the Nation of Islam home in New York. The request for Malcolm to move occurred after he announced his decision to leave the Nation of Islam. Angered by the eviction, Malcolm disclosed that Elijah Muhammad had extramarital affairs with his teenage secretaries, several of whom became pregnant for Muhammad. Malcolm went so far as to say that Elijah Muhammad was a religious faker. Out of anger, Malcolm misled the public, knowing that these were not extramarital affairs but that these women had become the wives of Elijah Muhammad (D. Muhammad, 2020).

In the Islamic world, it is not uncommon to have more than one wife. Elijah Muhammad had been ordered to take on wives, and he explained this in a letter to his son, Wallace D. Mohammed (personal letter to son Imam W. D. Mohammed). In 1993, Minister Louis Farrakhan, addressing the assassination of Malcolm X, allowed several of Elijah's wives to speak. They reported the following about Elijah Muhammad:

> Brothers and Sisters, I just want to say that all the years I worked with the Honorable Elijah Muhammad before he asked me to become his wife, there was never any kind of out of turn words, no sexual mistreatment— he treated us with the highest form of dignity and respect. —Evelyn Muhammad

> I bear witness that everything Elijah taught us about eating, cleaning and raising our children was true. —Ola Muhammad

> I know it's a pretty hard pill to swallow that the Honorable Elijah Muhammad took on wives. . . . He came to me, when I was very young, in a vision. I only saw his form never his face. But this vision lasted with me until I was a teenager and then after I heard Islam became prominent. —June Muhammad

The Honorable Elijah Muhammad is the most noble and virtuous and
moral man that you will ever know if you lived to be 1,000 or 2,000 years
old. —Tynnetta Muhammad (D. Muhammad, 2020, pp. 158–161)

The wives of Elijah Muhammad offered a counternarrative to the mainstream stories that have been told. An interesting story is that of June
Muhammad, who as a child had visions of Elijah Muhammad. This
means that these marriages were ordained before either had been born.
Elijah Muhammad's wives—like the Prophet Muhammad's wife Aisha,
who was young at the time of their marriage—played a major role in the
spread of Islam after his death.

Forty-six years after the death of Elijah Muhammad, his son Ishmael
Muhammad is now a national representative of Minister Louis Farrakhan. In 2021, he delivered the keynote address for the Nation of
Islam's Savior's Day Convention. It was the first time in forty years
that this address was not delivered by Minister Farrakhan. To date, all
of the children from Elijah Muhammad's first wife, Clara Muhammad,
have passed away, and it is his children from his other marriages who
live on to keep the Nation of Islam's legacy.

Time has born witness to the supreme wisdom and vision of Elijah
Muhammad. Those shaping the narrative around his domestic life
sought to slander him, and their writings were a form of yellow journalism. Yellow journalism includes sensationalizing stories that will attract
readers and are tabloid in nature, which includes a mixture of truth and
falsehood.

Dating back to 1959 (Wallace & Lomax, 1959) and the 1960s, when
the *Los Angeles Evening Herald-Examiner* wrote false claims about the
founder of the Nation of Islam in "The Black Merchants of Hate" (Balk
& Haley, 1963), the organization has been attacked for its attempt to
empower Black people to become free and independent.

Not only has the domestic life of Elijah Muhammad been weaponized against the Nation of Islam, but the most egregious lie has been that
Elijah Muhammad ordered the killing of Malcolm X. Elijah Muhammad did not have the spirit to have anyone killed. He was deeply pained
when Malcolm left the Nation of Islam because he had taught Malcolm
like no other minister.

He loved Malcolm like a son and grieved over Malcolm's words. He
also knew from his study of scriptures Malcolm's role in history and
pointed it out in his book *The Fall of America*. Moreover, members of

the Nation of Islam are forbidden from carrying weapons of any sort. In addition, Elijah Muhammad ordered his followers to leave Malcolm alone.

With his home wiretapped and agents placed throughout the Nation of Islam (Allah, 2007; Gardell, 1996), if Elijah Muhammad had ordered the assassination, this would have been known by the FBI. They could have then charged Elijah Muhammad with the murder and then made him prove that he had no part in it. There was no evidence, only lies and propaganda that have been retold to dissuade Blacks from studying these profound teachings that grew Malcolm into an intellectual giant.

Minister Farrakhan, describing an out-of-body experience, shared that he heard a cry that he had never heard in life coming from Elijah Muhammad. He heard Muhammad crying out, "My son, my son!" Farrakhan referenced the story of Absalom and David in relationship to Malcolm X and Elijah Muhammad (Ekiye, 2013).

Throughout the history of the Nation of Islam, the organization has faced deadly attacks in numerous forms. Elijah Muhammad as the leader also suffered from people in the Nation of Islam who brought all sorts of problems and issues for him to resolve. He witnessed people who were once in love with the teachings turn away. Betty Muhammad (2002) noted that sometimes his pillow would be soaked in tears.

When Master Fard Muhammad told him, I am leaving you with the hardest job of any man that ever lived (J. Muhammad, 2020), he was telling him a profound truth about the suffering he would experience. And while there were moments of satisfaction and joy at achieving many successes, he suffered for over forty years.

In February 1975, when he was brought to Mercy Hospital, it was not expected that he would pass away. The last words he spoke to his grandson Jesus Muhammad Ali were, "Why can't they figure out what is wrong with me?" (StreamingChurch Archives, 2018). Suffering from heart congestion that sped up his heartbeat, on February 25, the Most Honorable Elijah Muhammad gave up the ghost.

His protector, Wali Bahar, was asked by Elijah Muhammad's son Wallace D. Mohammed if he wanted to take a look at him in that state (CROE TV, 2018). Wali agreed and was shaken to find his beloved leader's eyes and mouth open. He closed his eyes but could not close his mouth. Wali—like Elijah's devoted followers—was shocked, distraught, and rendered lost by the death of Elijah Muhammad.

By the time of his death, the little man from rural Georgia, a share-cropper's son, had transformed the lives of countless people from various racial and ethnic groups. He reshaped Black thought and caused a whole generation of Black youth to refer to themselves as "brothers" and "sisters."

The term "Black" replaced "Negro" and "Afro-American." Elijah Muhammad removed the curse of being Black. In popular culture, artists like James Brown picked up on his teachings and declared, "I am Black and I am proud." Elijah Muhammad took an unlearned people and grew them into intellectual giants. His star pupils—Minister Malcolm X, Muhammad Ali, Imam Warith D. Mohammed, Tynnetta Muhammad, Minister Silas Muhammad, John Ali, and Minister Louis Farrakhan—were reflections of the knowledge espoused by Elijah Muhammad.

While many believe Elijah Muhammad died in 1975, there are those who believe he is still alive. Minister Farrakhan, at the 1981 Savior's Day Convention, declared Elijah Muhammad was alive, and this is the foundation he used to bring back the Nation of Islam after its fall in 1975. Jabril Muhammad (2012), a noted historian of the Nation of Islam, wrote,

> The second time period began on February 22, 1981. That's when Minister Farrakhan announced before approximately 3,000 people that the Honorable Elijah Muhammad was in fact alive. Minister Farrakhan began to spread this fact throughout America. He increasingly was bringing his teacher back to life in the minds and hearts of a growing number of people.

In 1989, at a national press conference, he shared an experience on the Mother Plane with Elijah Muhammad that occurred on September 17, 1985. During that 1989 press conference in what was called "The Announcement," Farrakhan (1989) disclosed to American leaders their plans to destroy Libya and the Nation of Islam. He told these leaders that he received this information from Elijah Muhammad on the Wheel. The experience of Minister Farrakhan does not seem to be an anomaly, as others have reported similar experiences that have caused them to believe Elijah Muhammad is alive (Ooyiman, 2020).

CONCLUSION

Elijah Muhammad's mission was to resurrect the mentally dead Blacks in America, and he eloquently noted that they had to be completely reeducated. His first encounter with law enforcement officials occurred in 1934 when he took Muslim children out of the Detroit public schools and placed them in the Muhammad University of Islam (E. Muhammad, 1965).

The arrest of Muslims for attempting to control their own education demonstrated that education was a major concern for those ruling society. The Whites who were shaping Black education were not educating for freedom but were training Black children to be more useful laborers for the owners of industry (Spivey, 2007).

Elijah Muhammad (1965), in his book *Message to the Blackman in America*, wrote that the Whites who were designing the education of Black people would not teach them the science of warfare, chemistry, and mating. Today most people have not grasped Elijah Muhammad's teachings, particularly as they relate to the sciences. For the most part, a major area of his teachings addresses military science, which is where the greatest scientific discoveries are housed. The hiding of knowledge has been one of the ways those in the dominant positions have been able to maintain their rule.

Elijah Muhammad (1965) pointed out that Senator Henry Berry declared that those ruling the society were hoping to keep certain bodies of knowledge away from Blacks in order relegate them to the life of a beast: "If we could extinguish the capacity to see the light, our work would be complete; they would then be on the level with the beast of the field and we should be safe" (p. 186). With only a fourth-grade education, Elijah Muhammad began his critique of education arguing that the education Blacks were receiving did not teach them the knowledge of self; thus, their creativity had yet to be unleashed. God was asleep in the Black man and woman, and it was knowledge that they needed to raise them from a mentally dead state.

This also meant changing their diet because it was food that was killing their mental capacities. They were taught to throw away intoxicating drinks and tobacco products. Instead of drinking alcohol, they were taught to drink from the word of God, which is like milk, purified to give them spiritual fortitude. It was this prescription that made his students lights in the midst of darkness.

Today, with all the rhetoric around social justice, diversity, and equity in education, one of the most extraordinary teachers in human history has been purposefully excluded from education discourse. Like all the prophets and messengers from history, he has been subjugated to a flood of lies and propaganda that have sought to hide knowledge emanating from him that would give birth to a new civilization.

To ensure his teachings do not touch the masses, the media have portrayed him in a negative way. Most notable in this flood of propaganda is that he was responsible for the assassination of Malcolm X. FBI documents detail the efforts that the federal government undertook to have stories placed in newspapers to discredit Elijah Muhammad and the Nation of Islam (D. Muhammad, 2020).

For over forty-four years, most writers have used these false narratives, along with his domestic life, to declare that he was immoral and a religious faker (Evanzz, 2001). The propaganda around the assassination of Malcolm X has been discussed in detail by Dr. Wesley Muhammad (T. Muhammad, 2021a). And the plurality of Elijah Muhammad's wives was discussed by Minister Louis Farrakhan (1993).

Dr. Wesley Muhammad has painstakingly researched the intricate details around the assassination of Malcolm X. In an interview with NFA Studios, he gave a detailed account of the assassination of Malcolm X, clearly showing that Elijah Muhammad had nothing to do with it (T. Muhammad, 2021a).

With regard to the domestic life of Elijah Muhammad, Minister Farrakhan in 1993 allowed some of his wives to speak about their relationship with him. The theme that emerged from their proclamations was the exemplary character and moral uprightness of Elijah Muhammad. The narratives that these wives shared ran counter to the majoritarian narratives that have been used to blemish his character.

Steven Biko declared that education is the most powerful weapon in the hands of the oppressed (cited in Chiwanza, 2017). This is most evident in Elijah Muhammad's teachings, making him a threat to national security. Why? Because he declared God appeared and bequeathed to him a knowledge that frees the whole of humanity from the adversary that is causing human suffering. This suffering is a direct result of the ideology that is undergirding society.

One example of this is the human capitalist ideology that is driving educational policy. Human capitalist ideology maintains that schools should be preparing students for work (Spring, 2011). This would explain why yesteryear's philanthropists spent more money on education than the US government (Gatto, 2017). And it would also explain the numerous think tanks and foundations that spend millions of dollars to shape educational policy in the twenty-first century (Spring, 2011).

Elijah Muhammad rose from humble beginnings in Sandersville, Georgia, with only a fourth-grade education to become a world shaper (Berg, 2009). In his Table Talks, he described it best when he said, "Nobody there was looking at me plowing a mule thought that I would ever be a Scientist teaching the world" (S. Muhammad, 2012, p. 122). The entire scope of Elijah Muhammad's mission was education. His teachings set ablaze all these new education gimmicks designed to keep people enslaved. His teachings are paving the way for a new world, and as he said, "No education of this world of the white race will be accepted into the new world" (E. Muhammad, 1974, p. 124).

Chapter Four

The Teachings

While much has been written about Elijah Muhammad, there has not been an in-depth focus on what he taught. To begin, Elijah Muhammad did not have a teaching per se but was delivering a message that included a teaching that he received from the man he called Master Fard Muhammad. During the three years and four months that Elijah Muhammad spent under the tutelage of Master Fard Muhammad, he was taught something about everything in the universe (E. Muhammad, 2006; J. Muhammad, 1996). The number of areas that these teachings covered is too voluminous to list in this chapter.

However, most scholars writing about Elijah Muhammad either have not taken the time to study what he taught or have not been able to fully comprehend these teachings. In addition, most of these writers only focus on what he taught about the origin of the races. His disclosure of the origin of the races was one component of what he taught. For example, he taught about sun storms long before anybody knew about such phenomena (Muhammad, 2006). With only a fourth-grade education, he declared that water could be likened to God because it could not be produced or destroyed (E. Muhammad, 1993a, p. 16).

The real power of Elijah Muhammad was in the body of knowledge that he disclosed. The Southern Poverty Law Center (2021) has listed the Nation of Islam as a hate group because of its teachings about race. The "hate group" label has caused educators to turn a blind eye to a model of education that has transformed Black lives. Contrary to the claims of racist teachings, one could argue that what Elijah Muhammad new science that has now emerged in the form of new technological advancements. Diangelo (2018) wrote that when Blacks speak forcefully about White supremacy and racism, they are cast by Whites as being reverse racists.

It could be argued that Elijah Muhammad's teachings should be a litmus test for those claiming to be advocates of social justice. Elijah Muhammad offered a liberation pedagogy to address the problems facing Black communities. His vision was to create an independent nation, and he articulated a path toward true freedom for Blacks in America.

The Nation of Islam did not depend on those who were ruling the country for financial support. They were engaged in buying land, setting up businesses, and developing an economic infrastructure that would free them of begging from the "White man."

A major component of what Elijah Muhammad taught about education was connected to capitalism. He pointed out that the education of Blacks in America did not prepare them to be independent because they had to rely for jobs on those who were ruling society. Long before Bowles and Gintis (1976) pointed out the role of capitalism in American education, Elijah Muhammad wrote that the education of Blacks in America did not equip them with the idea to produce jobs for themselves. He taught economic independence because Black labor was under White control:

> Since our being brought in chains to the shores of America, our brain power, labor, skills, talent and wealth have been taken, given and spent toward building and adding to the civilization of another people. It is time for you and me, the so-called Negroes, to start doing for ourselves. (E. Muhammad, 1965, p. 56)

For those waxing rich from Black labor, Elijah Muhammad became their adversary because he showed Blacks how to pool their resources to become independent.

He taught that to be independent, Blacks needed to own land. From land ownership, they could produce all the necessities to survive. Agricultural education was important to him because he realized that oppressed people needed to produce their own food (Muhammad, 1965). The same critique that he applied to education included reasons for agricultural education.

Several historically Black colleges and universities (HBCUs) were founded as agricultural colleges, and the majority are in the South, where Blacks have acquired large tracts of land. Unfortunately, the teachings of Elijah Muhammad are not studied by administrators at HBCUs, and they do not take an African-centered perspective in leading these universities. In part, the selection of leaders for some of these universities is done by majority-White administrative boards that supersede university search committees.

By owning land and controlling resources for their basic needs, Blacks would outgrow the stress of procuring food, clothing, and shelter. Fulfilling these basic needs would become like breathing air. The materials from the earth would be embellished by their creative genius. For example, certain types of material would be extracted from the earth to produce new automobiles. In one of the most profound interviews given by Elijah Muhammad with Buzz Anderson, he discussed how the wisdom of God is transferred (Truth/Controversy, 2020).

He says, for example, that if you look at this recording material that you are using, if you comeback years later, you will find that it has been improved from its original state. He goes on to say that after so many years, if the originator of the recorder returned, he would no longer recognize it. Elijah Muhammad envisioned an advanced society and had an inkling of a world that no eye had ever seen. To bring that world into existence, human development would be required.

Human development begins with awakening the divine essence in the human being, which produces lifelong learners and grows its adherents into a oneness with the creator. By awakening the divine essence, the creative mind becomes active, birthing ideas. This in turn leads to taking an idea out of one's mind and making it a reality. Elijah Muhammad (1993d) wrote, "If this house is sitting in my mind but it is not yet built and I can bring it out of my mind into reality, that's the God" (pp. 51–52). Making ideas tangible made him successful.

Today it could be argued that scholars in universities are giving birth to these teachings. When exploring many of the leading theoretical frameworks in education, one will find similarities to what Elijah Muhammad taught in the 1930s. This chapter reviews Elijah Muhammad's teachings in the context of educational theory, exploring critical pedagogy, critical race theory (CRT), and critical Whiteness studies.

The chapter infuses the political, economic, and spiritual components of what Elijah Muhammad taught.

CRITICAL PEDAGOGY

Critical pedagogy is an educational framework that seeks to empower those who are oppressed. The term "critical pedagogy" was first coined in the 1980s and has since been developed by Henry Giroux and others (Giroux, 2010; Darder et al., 2017). Peter McLaren (2015) wrote, "Critical pedagogy is fundamentally concerned with understanding the relationship between power and knowledge" (p. 144). Its leading architect, Paulo Freire (2018), laid the groundwork for what is now known as critical pedagogy. His classic *Pedagogy of the Oppressed* has influenced the ideas of countless scholars in the field of education and theology.

The Great Depression deeply affected Freire, causing his family to experience poverty. When his family's fortunes improved, he could continue his joy of learning, which eventually led to him earn a law degree (Stevens, 2012). He never practiced law but became devoted to the study of education after marrying Elza Maia Costa de Oliveira, a schoolteacher (Bentley, 1999).

His early life experiences and his interest in education shaped his ideas about the intersection of education and poverty. In 1961, he was appointed director of the Department of Cultural Extension at the University of Recife, where he developed a literacy program with adult learners that had them reading in forty-five days (Oxman, 2017).

After the overthrow of the Brazilian government, he was arrested for seventy days and labeled a traitor. In 1968, his book *Pedagogy of the Oppressed* was well received and resulted in him landing a teaching position at Harvard University (Oxman, 2017). Freire's writings have influenced a cadre of scholars in education (Darder et al., 2017). The scholars of critical pedagogy have provided scholarship that critiques, disrupts, and deconstructs what it means to be educated.

Antonio Darder and colleagues (2017), in *The Critical Pedagogy Reader*, compiled articles from the leading scholars on critical pedagogy. The reader traces the origin of critical pedagogy and can be helpful to educators seeking to empower students to become active agents of change.

Joe Kincheloe (2008), in his book *Critical Pedagogy: A Primer*, described critical pedagogy as "being dedicated to resisting the harmful effects of dominant power" (p. 34). Darder (2015) wrote that critical pedagogy also addresses developing a critical consciousness in students: "Accordingly, a humanizing vision of pedagogy nurtures critical consciousness" (p. 64). She goes on to highlight that critical consciousness can inspire students to become creative.

Critical pedagogues also discuss the role of self-determination for oppressed people (Karenga, 2002). *Self-determination* entails those from oppressed groups taking on the agency to determine what is in their best interest. Through self-determination, those from oppressed groups are not beholden to the ideology of those ruling the society.

While much of the focus on critical pedagogy is centered around the Frankfurt School of thought, there has always been a critical Black pedagogy (CBP). Throughout the Black experience in the Americas, there were Black leaders who vehemently fought against White supremacy and racism. Pitre (2019) wrote that critical Black pedagogy entails the following: (1) African-centered perspective, (2) multicultural education, (3) critical pedagogy, and (4) African American spirituality.

In regard to an African-centered perspective, Reiland Rabaka (2006) wrote, "Africana critical theory is a theory of critical domination and discrimination in classical and contemporary, continental and diaspora African life world's and live experiences" (p. 133). Whereas Africana critical theory does not focus on the phenotype of its advocates, critical Black pedagogy lifts the voices of Black thought leaders to prominence.

In Freire's (2018) *Pedagogy of the Oppressed*, there are several quotes that are similar to Elijah Muhammad's critique of Black education. Table 4.1 presents some examples.

Prior to Freire's 1968 publication of *Pedagogy of the Oppressed*, Elijah Muhammad (1965) published the classic book *Message to the Blackman in America*. The book was in fact a *pedagogy of liberation* that laid the foundation for complete freedom for those languishing under White domination, and it informed liberation theology. The case can be made that Black leaders were the forerunners of critical pedagogy (Pitre, 2019). Both Elijah Muhammad and Carter G. Woodson (1999) had been teaching critically for thirty-plus years before Freire's monumental work.

Table 4.1.

Elijah Muhammad's Critiques	Paulo Freire's (2018) Critiques
"When rightly viewed, your education has been designed by your oppressors with the specific intent of keeping you in servitude." (1973, p. 11)	"Education as the exercise of domination stimulates the credulity of students, with the ideological intent (often not perceived by educators) of indoctrinating them to adopt to the world of oppression."
"The slave-master will not teach you the knowledge of self, as there would not be a master-slave relationship any longer." (1965, p. 37)	"The oppressed, having internalized the image of the oppressor and adopted their guidelines, are fearful of freedom."
"When you stand up and speak a word in behalf of your own people, you are classified as a troublemaker, you are classified as a Communist, as a race hater and everything but good." (1973, p. 6)	"Never in history has violence been initiated by the oppressed. How could they be the initiators, if they themselves are a result of violence."
"There is much misunderstanding among us because of our inferior knowledge of self. We have been to schools where they do not teach the knowledge of self. We have been to the schools of our slave master children." (1965, p. 34)	"Self-depreciation is another characteristic of the oppressed, which derives from their internalization of the opinion the oppressors hold of them."
"Separation of the so-called Negroes from their slave masters' children is a must. It is the only solution to our problem." (1965, p. 45).	"The solution is not to integrate them into the structure of oppression, but to transform that structure so that they can be become beings for themselves."

In the case of Elijah Muhammad, he built an entire nation through a reeducation program that proved it could take the most unlearned of Black people and make them intellectual and spiritual giants. Elijah Muhammad created universities across the United States that demonstrated the heights that Black students could reach.

His approach to education began with a view that each human being has a divine essence that needs to be awakened and cultivated. His education program was designed to raise the God-consciousness in Blacks, which in turn would stimulate ideas that would lead to the birthing of a new world. Today's educators are disturbed when the term "God" is used in an educational context.

They believe that mentioning God in the context of education is a violation of the separation of church and state. In part because educators rarely read literature about the philosophy of education, they are unaware that at the root of educational practices are philosophies about religion and God. For example, Ozmon and Craver (2008), throughout their book *Philosophical Foundations of Education*, highlighted the intersection between education, philosophy, and religion.

The lack of discourse around spirituality and education has led educators to resemble technical workers who never discover the deeper meaning of what it means to educate. Giroux (2020) cogently wrote, "Teachers in the public school system fare no better than university educators, as they are increasingly deskilled, reduced to either technicians or security guards, or both."

Peter McLaren (2015) alluded to the deskilling of teachers and argued that Western epistemological assumptions are undergirding educational practices. These Western ideologies are in contrast to educational philosophies that are spiritual. For Black people, education is a spiritual undertaking. In consonance with the Africana tradition, Elijah Muhammad (1965) began his education program with the study of God, positing that he is a human being:

> God is a man and we just cannot make Him other than man, lest we make Him an inferior one; for man's intelligence has no equal in other than man. His wisdom is infinite; capable of accomplishing anything that His brain can conceive. A spirit is subjected to us and not we to the spirit. (p. 5)

Elijah Muhammad connected God to education when he mentioned intelligence, wisdom, and the brain. Scholars in the field of neuroscience are exploring neurotheology, which is a study of the impact that religion has on the brain (Newberg & Waldman, 2009). In addition to discussing education in a spiritual context, Elijah Muhammad disrupted deficit thinking about human potential, arguing that there is no limit to what human beings can achieve.

In other writings, he said that the impossible was destroyed when God created himself (E. Muhammad, 1992). After creating the self, he (God) began studying the self and started bringing into creation other forms of life. He made a law (Allah—All Law) that all living things can create themselves. Biologists call this self-autopoiesis (Pitre, 2018).

Elijah Muhammad, in teaching that God is a man, did not contradict biblical passages that depicted God as a human being. One example comes from Philippians 2:7–8, which states, regarding Jesus,

> But made himself of no reputation, and took upon him the form of a servant, and was made in the likeness of men: And being found in fashion as a man, he humbled himself, and became obedient unto death, even the death of the cross. (KJV)

When Elijah Muhammad declared that God is a man, he was highlighting the agency of human beings to direct their lives. He taught Blacks not to wait on a mystery God because they had the power to change their condition. In the problem book of the Nation of Islam, he asked, "Will you sit at home and wait for a mystery God to bring you food?" (E. Muhammad, 1993c, p. 18).

And his response was "emphatically no," that they who had tried the mystery God were left hungry, naked, and without a home (E. Muhammad, 1993c, p. 18). Freire (2018) also wrote that the oppressed are taught to passively accept their oppression as the will of God. Giroux (2020) wrote that critical pedagogy not only is about telling the truth but also involves acting. Freire (2018) wrote that the oppressed must learn of their agency to transform unjust social arrangements.

Elijah Muhammad declared that the knowledge of self was missing in the education of Blacks in America. Having been stripped of the knowledge of their ancestral history, Blacks in America, through the education process, were taught that their Blackness was a curse (Woodson, 1999). The curriculum that Blacks were provided after the Civil War did not consider literature from the African or Eastern canon.

The curriculum was carefully constructed to make sure Blacks would not acquire knowledge of themselves. Elijah Muhammad said that the worst crime committed against Blacks in America was stripping and depriving them of the knowledge of self. He declared, "Robbing a man of the knowledge of self is the worst sin that be committed against any human being" (cited in Pitre, 2007, p. 182).

Elijah Muhammad's position regarding the knowledge of self aligns with questions raised by scholars of curriculum. For example, who decides what is placed in the curriculum? And whose knowledge is taught in schools? With only a fourth-grade education, Elijah Muhammad (1965) responded to these questions of curriculum, saying,

> We have been to schools where they do not teach us the knowledge of self. We have been to the schools of our slave-masters children. We have been to their schools and gone as far as they allowed us to go. That was not far enough for us to learn a knowledge of self. (p. 34)

Elijah Muhammad argued that it was the lack of knowledge of self that caused Blacks in America to see themselves as an inferior people. Without the knowledge of self, they could be taught of the greatness of Europeans, which in turn led to the fatalism described by Freire (2018):

> Self-deprecation is another characteristic of the oppressed, which derives from their internalization of the opinion the oppressors hold of them. So often they hear that they are good for nothing, know nothing and are incapable of learning anything—that they are sick, lazy, and unproductive—that in the end they become convinced of their own unfitness. (p. 63)

In today's schools, the educational discourse is centered around a so-called achievement gap between Black and White students (T. Howard, 2020). The achievement gap becomes a way to skillfully imply that something is inherently wrong with Black students. Critical race theorists have argued that high-stakes testing is a form of racism (Ladson-Billings, 2021).

The achievement gap rhetoric has resulted in more accountability measures. High accountability is reinforced in public schools where Black and Brown students are the majority. These heightened measures form the bedrock for teaching methods that are based on memorization and regurgitation to improve test scores. Martin Haberman (1991) called this a pedagogy of poverty because it stifles student creativity. The test-score frenzy is a skillful way to gain more control over what is taught and how it is taught.

The genius of Black children is being put to death under yesteryear's eugenics movement. Those ruling the society have manufactured an educational crisis (Berliner & Biddle, 1995), and they have skillfully weaponized the education of Black students. Woodson (1999) described weaponized education when he said that to teach a person that his race is a curse is the worst sort of lynching.

CRITICAL BLACK PEDAGOGY FOR TEACHERS

Previous sections of this book have discussed teacher preparation, but this section reviews critical Black pedagogy in more detail. Critical Black pedagogy was framed because of the absence of Black thought leaders in the educational discourse.

The educational philosophies used to prepare future educators are primarily from European scholars. There is virtually no discussion of Black thought leaders who critiqued and offered models of education for Black children.

The new wave of preparing educators in major universities has been centered around addressing issues of diversity, equity, and social justice. However, future teachers very seldom read about critical Black pedagogues who were successful in transforming *Black lives*, particularly Elijah Muhammad.

Critical Black pedagogy includes preparing educators to understand what it means to have an African-centered perspective when teaching. Asante (1991) offered a definitive work on what it means to include an African-centered perspective in the educational discourse. Educators who are trained with an African-centered perspective will more likely be able to overcome deficit thinking, and they will provide a more culturally relevant pedagogy to students.

The second component of CBP is multicultural education. The preparation of teachers by way of multicultural education provides future educators with multiple perspectives for teaching and assessing diverse students. It also offers a way to holistically critique educational practice. It draws from the work of James Banks (2019) and other scholars of multicultural education.

The third tenet of CBP is critical pedagogy. Under critical pedagogy, the work of Paulo Freire and others is reviewed. Since critical pedagogy is primarily concerned with empowering oppressed groups, it aligns with the educational critiques of several Black thought leaders (Asante, 1991; Du Bois, 1903; Muhammad, 1965; Woodson, 1999).

Lastly, African American spirituality is included because education for Black people is spiritual (Akbar, 1998). The current educational practice is based on European materialism, which does not value cultivating the soul. For Africana people, education and religion are connected, and they form the foundation for spirituality in education. It was in the churches that Blacks were free to create a unique educational experience that allowed them to unleash their creativity.

Critical Black pedagogy offers educators the opportunity to review thoughtful critiques, ideas, and solutions for the improvement of Black education.

DECONSTRUCTING DOMINANT IDEOLOGIES

Elijah Muhammad offered an educational model that could be used to retrain teachers. Moreover, his model could be used to disrupt deficit thinking. The current educational system, through its laws and policies, certifies teachers who can maintain White rule without the teachers ever knowing that this is an underlying goal of those ruling society. The training of educators (teachers and administrators) does not prepare them to disrupt these systems but in fact makes them complicit in perpetuating educational inequities (Pitre & Smith-Gray, 2020). Likewise, educators who are conscious and attempt to address these inequities might be punished by school boards who are entrenched in White supremacist ideology.

An example of this occurred when a principal who asked teachers to read Peggy McIntosh's (1998) *White Privilege* was removed from the school after White teachers complained to the school board (Fine, 2019). In another example, a teacher who used critical and culturally relevant pedagogy to transform a rural school plagued with gang fights and student apathy encountered White parents and teachers who were upset that he included an African-centered perspective in the study of American history (Pitre, 2011). The teacher's life was threatened, and he was later transferred from the school despite having a positive impact on all the students.

Additionally, the media glorifies drug dealers and gangster images, selling these to Black youth. They have crafted an image of Blacks as bestial and savage to the degree that record labels promote these images (W. Muhammad, 2017). In turn, corporate giants are creating a culture that criminalizes Black youth without them ever knowing they are being prepared for self-destruction. Words like "beast," "savage," and "ghetto" are glamorized. Elijah Muhammad (1967) vehemently argued that education banishes savagery and said, "We are carried by the evil scientists of this world and we must fight back" (p. 4).

Henry Giroux (2020) identified this as public pedagogy, highlighting how media images impact what occurs in schools. Public pedagogy is a form of social engineering. In the 1990s, Minister Louis Farrakhan, a student of Elijah Muhammad, traveled across the United States to address the disproportionate incarceration of Black men. He also addressed the fratricide of Black men on "Stop the Killing" tours and in "Men's Only" meetings, informing Black men that they were being played by those ruling society.

Michelle Alexander's (2012) *The New Jim Crow* mirrored what Minister Farrakhan had been saying for years regarding Black males being overly incarcerated. The Nation of Islam, through its teachings, disrupted the public pedagogy or images of Black men as criminals by using historical truths to demonstrate that Blacks are not inferior but are the original people whence all people came to exist (Farrakhan, 2009). In sharing this knowledge, Farrakhan used theology to support his arguments. Unlike in the European construction of education, which compartmentalizes the disciplines, in the Nation of Islam, theology and education appear together.

Elijah Muhammad began his education program by deconstructing theology, the source from which the education world is built. He taught that being Black is not a curse but is the source from which all things came to exist. The knowledge of self would require Blacks to study the ancient civilizations that predated European civilization. He taught that Blacks had civilizations that were superior to those of Europeans (E. Muhammad, 1965).

According to Muhammad's teachings, the Black man is the original man and the wisest being that exists in the universe but has been made blind, deaf, and dumb to allow White rule for a six-thousand-year period. Additionally, he taught that Blacks have no birth record because no one was present to document their beginning over sixty-six trillion years ago. The study of cosmology and astronomy holds the secrets of Black men's wisdom (E. Muhammad, 1974, 2006)

He taught that the planets are live eggs that Black scientists created, and there is life on all these planets. Pluto represented the Black man in America because it is so far from the sun that scientists believe no life can exist on it because it is a frozen planet (E. Muhammad, 1974).

But Elijah Muhammad declared that the Black man, like Pluto, while appearing frozen in mental death, with just a touch of light, meaning knowledge, will begin rotating.

The planet Mars intrigued him, and he taught that the people on Mars are Black people. They live underground and live a thousand earth years. In the 1930s, the general population dismissed his teachings about Mars as foolishness, but scientists have followed up on these teachings and are trying to discover if there is life on Mars. Elijah Muhammad (1997) wrote,

> Now they have also given us pictures of Mars, a planet that have life on it, they have been peeping in the window of Mars that life there looks near like us. Men growing seven and nine feet tall, from seven to nine feet tall and living a thousand of our earth years. (p. 63)

In July 2020, scientists launched *Perseverance* to explore Mars for signs of life. Elijah Muhammad's critical pedagogy was interdisciplinary, and this is what makes him a threat to those ruling society. His teachings spark in students the thirst for knowledge. This caused him to say, "Knowledge of self makes you take on the great virtue of learning" (E. Muhammad, 1965, p. 39).

The knowledge of self is excluded from the curriculum that most Black students encounter in public schools. With regard to Black History Month, Elijah Muhammad wrote that it does not teach the accomplishments of Black people beyond the American experience. And when it does mention Blacks, its focus aligns with the narrative of those ruling society.

In his critique of education, he pointed out that the destruction of the Eurocentric educational system was the best thing that could happen because it would free Blacks from the mental chains that were not allowing them to tap the uniqueness of their being (E. Muhammad, 1973). Freire (2018) similarly wrote the oppressed are not marginalized but are within the structures and systems that oppress them.

The goal, he writes, is to transform those structures. For Elijah Muhammad, the purpose of God's coming was not to transform but to fulfill scripture wherein it talks about God making all things new. In *Our Savior Has Arrived*, he provided a glimpse of what education in the new world will entail:

"First He Makes a New Mind for us and a New Way of thinking." He teaches us a different education, one that we have never had before. He Gives us Education on the Wisdom, Knowledge, and Understanding of Gods . . . not of prophets . . . but of the Gods of the Prophets of the past. He builds our minds according to the way Gods Think and not the way of thinking of servants (prophets). (E. Muhammad, 1974, p. 123)

This knowledge of the gods of the prophets becomes the basis for a new curriculum, and it grows the human being into something new. In the new world, the present education system will be of no value. Muhammad (1974) wrote, "However no education of this world of the White race will be accepted into the new world. For the new world you have a new education and government" (p. 24).

While critical pedagogues offer a critique of educational policies and practices, Elijah Muhammad offered a body of knowledge that raised the consciousness of diverse groups of people. His teachings inspired many people to become avid readers, and his students became idols to the downtrodden Blacks. They were not seeking to play sports or entertain but were now active agents in bringing to birth a world opposite of the "White man's" world. Out of Elijah Muhammad's teaching came the push for Black studies, which led to ethnic studies and now the current multicultural education/diversity studies.

James Banks (1972), considered the father of multicultural education, in his earlier works in the 1970s was focused on the Black self-concept. The ideas he expressed have similarities to the teachings of Elijah Muhammad. In his widely read *An Introduction to Multicultural Education*, Banks (2019) mentions freedom, justice, and equality, which are the tenets of the Nation of Islam's teachings.

Elijah Muhammad was a forerunner of critical pedagogy and multicultural education, and he offered a body of knowledge that reshaped Black thought. It also paved the way for many popular theoretical frameworks such as critical race theory.

CRITICAL RACE THEORY

Critical race theory was born when a group of critical legal scholars became upset with the slow pace of legal reform in the United States (Delgado & Stefancic, 2017). Moreover, they believed the legal critiques emphasized class struggles to the detriment of racial discourse. Derek Bell, considered the father of critical race theory, was influenced by Malcolm X's Black nationalist ideology.

In his well-known book *Faces at the Bottom of the Well: The Permanence of Racism*, Bell (1992) devoted an entire section to discussion of Minister Louis Farrakhan. Bell (1992) wrote, "Well, perhaps the best contemporary example of the Fourth Rule involves the adverse reaction of many whites to the Muslim minister Louis Farrakhan. Smart and super articulate, Minister Farrakhan is perhaps the best living example of a black man ready, willing, and able to 'tell it like it is' regarding who is responsible for racism in this country" (p. 118). He also mentioned the courageousness of Malcolm X for not only speaking the truth but also acting on that truth. Both Malcolm X and Louis Farrakhan were students of Elijah Muhammad, so in reality it is Elijah Muhammad's teachings that were influential in the formation of critical race theory.

In the field of education, Gloria Ladson-Billings and William Tate (1995) wrote the seminal article on critical race theory in education. They explored Whiteness as a form of property that gave Whites advantages in schools. Ladson-Billings in other writings highlighted the role of race in curricula, instruction, assessment, school funding, and desegregation (Pitre et al., 2021).

Those familiar with Elijah Muhammad's teachings can clearly see the similarities to CRT (Abdullah, 2016). In fact, a careful reading of Ladson-Billings (1995) has disclosed that she is an extraordinary scholar who is knowledgeable about some aspects of Elijah Muhammad's teachings (Pitre et al., 2021).

Long before the term "critical race theory" was coined, Elijah Muhammad opined that Blacks were brought to America as property for those ruling the country (S. Muhammad, 2012). When he used the term "slave master," he was referring to a special class of Whites who owned the country. In his critique of these owners, he argued the worst crime they committed was stripping Blacks of the knowledge of self. After the Civil War, those governing society in the development of schools for Blacks in America did not intend to teach them the knowledge of self because it would make them a free and independent people.

Regarding legal issues, Elijah Muhammad pointed out that the US Constitution did not consider Blacks as human beings to be protected under its declarations (E. Muhammad, 1965). The laws that governed the United States were made to protect the interest of those with wealth and property. The American dream meant to own property, which meant Black people. The term "real estate" refers to living beings— Black people—and it was the acquisition of Blacks as property that gave Whites higher social status.

For his critique of White supremacy, Elijah Muhammad was labeled un-American. Giroux (2020) declared the same regarding teachers and scholars who offer critical perspectives being labeled as un-American in the twenty-first century. Elijah Muhammad's teachings caught the eye of J. Edgar Hoover, who placed informants and agents inside the Nation of Islam (Gardell, 1996). Even members of Congress became involved to the degree that they were in the process of issuing a subpoena for Elijah Muhammad to appear before Congress for his supposed anti-American teaching. In fact, it was the school that the fact-finding commission was concerned about, and it drew the following response from Elijah Muhammad (1965):

> Recently, the California State Senate Fact-Finding Subcommittee on Un-American Activities, in their "Eleventh Report" to the 1961 Regular California Legislature, in Sacramento, California, on pages 131–138 under the heading "THE NEGRO MUSLIMS," are charging us with being un-American, that we now operate a school for the indoctrination of young Negroes with race hatred. (This is untrue, for we only teach them who you really are. They can hate or love you, it is up to them.) You have always had private schools. First, your students not only learn to hate Negroes but are the number one murderers of Negroes. Second, we do not teach them to disregard their family names—they do NOT KNOW them. We teach them to discard YOUR family NAMES and get their real Nation's names, for your names are not our legal names! (p. 177)

Elijah Muhammad would later respond to the label "un-American" by saying,

> Un-American: I wish to prove, according to the English language, that every so-called Negro, Indian and all nonwhite Europeans are un-American according to the dictionary's definition of an American. An American according to the dictionary "is a citizen of the United States or of the earlier British Colonies; one not belonging to one of the aboriginal races." We belong to the aboriginal nation of the earth; the White or European race is not aboriginal. (p. 183)

Critical race theorists have mentioned that race and racism are permanent fixtures in American life. They argue that racism is built into the fabric of American jurisprudence, but it was Elijah Muhammad who articulated—years before CRT—that Blacks would not receive equal treatment under the law.

Regarding the curriculum, Elijah Muhammad knew that the true history of Blacks would not be taught in public schools. The curriculum would only include Blacks when it benefited White interest. Peter McLaren (2015) wrote that determining what is included in the curriculum is a political act and that certain forms of knowledge are valued over others.

Elijah Muhammad (1965, 1973 2006) referred to this as the hiding of knowledge, and this is what made him adamant that Blacks should control their education. The curriculum became a contested space for Elijah Muhammad because he sought to raise the consciousness of Black people by teaching them the knowledge of God and self. For Elijah Muhammad, God was not a spook but a real live human being who had superior knowledge.

Moreover, he claimed the Supreme Being taught him the requisite knowledge needed to restore Blacks in America back to their original selves (E. Muhammad, 1965, 1973, 1974, 2006). When Dr. Martin Luther King Jr. met Elijah Muhammad in 1966, he was probably stunned to hear such knowledge.

Elijah Muhammad's words may have affected Dr. King, as a student of theology, to the degree that he was beginning to see the salvation of Black people in a biblical context, and this may have led him to express his mountaintop experience, where he declared he had been to the mountaintop. Was this mountaintop Elijah Muhammad?

The knowledge that Elijah Muhammad brought infused a criticality across disciplines and caused his students to have a higher degree of knowledge than those who held doctoral degrees at universities. For example, when he taught that the pyramids were built by Black people, he also taught that these pyramids were aligned with two stars and that in order to destroy them, you would have to destroy the stars that they are aligned to (Malcolm X, 2019). At the time, this was new information to those ruling society.

Today it is clear that Elijah Muhammad's teachings stretched across disciplines. If we were to place him in the context of a university organization, he could be a dean in the following colleges: education, business, social and behavioral science, medicine, agriculture, arts and humanities, engineering, architecture, science, and technology (Pitre, 2021a).

Realizing that Black children would experience a curriculum that did not teach them the knowledge of self, he started universities of Islam. He was purposeful in claiming that they were universities, not schools, because they taught a university knowledge.

The curriculum in these universities sought to have students complete their doctoral studies by the time they were eighteen years old. He chimed, "Teach them fast." The university did not require students to be in school eight hours a day. But instead, they spent around twenty hours a week in seat time (E. Muhammad, 2012). Students would visit various professions to gain experience.

In today's education system, this is similar to conducting an internship. Elijah Muhammad in the 1930s was a forerunner in including internships in the learning experience. Imagine what it would be like to include internships in K-12 schools.

Regarding instruction, he was the master of culturally relevant pedagogy. Culturally relevant pedagogy has three main tenets: academic competence, cultural competence, and critical consciousness (Ladson-Billings, 1995). Long before the term "culturally relevant pedagogy" was coined, he believed in academic competence. He believed that educators held a very high place in society, and it was their job to prepare Black students for success. Academically, he believed the education of Black students should go beyond reading, writing, and arithmetic.

With regard to cultural competence, one of the tenets of culturally relevant pedagogy, Elijah Muhammad was a genius at connecting all the disciplines to the study of self. Disclosing truths about Black relevancy across disciplines made him an extraordinary teacher. Through his teaching, the Bible took on new meaning for his students.

The Bible became a foundation for disclosing in a collective way the plight of Blacks in America. As the Messenger of God, he was the interpreter of a message that would free Blacks from slavery and oppression. He articulated that God works in formula and then sends a messenger with interpretation of that formula. Elijah Muhammad's teaching was a forerunner of culturally relevant pedagogy, and it gave life to a people who were like dry bones, cut off from their origin.

Perhaps the greatest threat that Elijah Muhammad posed to those rul-ing society was in making Blacks conscious. While civil rights leaders were trying to integrate, Elijah Muhammad declared these initiatives would not lead to complete freedom. He argued that never in history had a slave owner made his slave an equal. He then demonstrated that through something simple like a name, Blacks in America remained the property of Whites.

Throwing off the slave master's name was a first step in being free. He then articulated that to be free, one needs to acquire land. This led him to develop a three-year economic program that would allow Blacks to pool their resources to buy land (E. Muhammad, 1965). From the land, they could produce all the necessities for their survival. This led him to set up a banking system that was modeled after those of success-ful European countries (E. Muhammad, 1965).

Clearly, he developed a consciousness in Blacks that led to the 1960s Freedom Movement and the many curriculum changes that occurred in K-12 and higher education. This also caused those in power to make concessions that would pacify Blacks. Critical race theorists refer to these concessions as interest convergence, when the interest of Whites converges with Black demands.

An example of interest convergence is the *Brown v. Board of Education of Topeka* ruling that required schools to be desegregated, which paved the way for disrupting Black consciousness and led to the elimination of Black teachers. Desegregation benefited White interest because their institutions could then nurture the best of Black talent. One example is in college athletics, where Blacks athletes have become the new gold.

They bring in millions of dollars to not only the universities but also local businesses. The business owners are connected to the politicians, who sanction racist policies that negatively impact Blacks. An example of this is the harsh sentencing laws that disproportionately affect Black men (Alexander, 2012). In the South, the racism is virulent, but south-ern football teams are using Black talent to wax rich.

Elijah Muhammad's critique of White dominance led him to say these nice gestures were tricks. Critical race theorists use the term "interest convergence," whereas Elijah Muhammad used the word "tric-knology," the science of using tricks to rule. Hegemony, like interest convergence, is when the oppressed give consent to their oppression without knowing it. McLaren (2015) wrote, "Hegemony is a struggle in which the powerful win the consent of those who are oppressed, with the oppressed unknowingly participating in their own oppression" (p. 140).

Critical race theory also entails counternarratives, including story-telling from the perspective of those whose voices have been silenced. Counternarratives disrupt the majoritarian stories that dominate schools and the larger society. Opposed to the Eurocentric perspective that America was founded on the ideals of freedom and justice, critical race theorists would point to the African holocaust that cost millions of Black lives (Hine et al., 2009).

Countering the majoritarian narrative, critical race theorists would also argue that American institutions were built on racism and White supremacy. White supremacy is so ingrained in American culture that it can be found in the games people play. One example of this is the game of pool, which represents White supremacy.

The white ball is the power ball, and the goal of the game is to knock the colored balls in the hole. The Black ball is the last ball to be knocked in the hole, which represents anti-Black racism. Through false narratives rooted in theology, psychology, education, history, and other disciplines, White supremacy could be maintained. Elijah Muhammad, through his articulation of the origin of life, disrupted the narratives that supported White supremacy.

He revealed profound truths about the origin of life, arguing that it began with the atom and resulted in the first human being, the Black man—the maker, the owner, the cream of the planet earth, the God of the universe (E. Muhammad, 1993c). Shattering White supremacy, he disclosed that the origin of the White man was a result of the Black man experimenting on the self (E. Muhammad, 1965, 1993c). An offshoot of critical race theory is critical White (or Whiteness) studies.

CRITICAL WHITE STUDIES

Critical White studies is the critique of Whiteness. It seeks to disrupt White supremacy by offering a historical analysis of how White supremacy has brought suffering to aboriginal people all over the earth. In *Race Traitor*, Ignatiev and Garvey (1996) contend that "the key to solving the social problems of our age is to abolish the white race. . . . So long as the white race exists, all movements against racism are doomed to fail" (p. 10).

In *Becoming and Unbecoming White: Owning and Disowning a Racial Identity*, a group of White scholars critiqued Whiteness, and one chapter by Christine Clark reviewed Janet E. Helms's racial identity stages and asked if Whites—after reaching a certain level on the scale— could become members of the Nation of Islam. Zeus Leonardo (2009) highlighted that "transforming whiteness also lacks history because it does not come to terms with the function of whiteness" (p. 131).

While the field of critical White studies has gained traction in the academy, the man who offered one of the most potent critiques of Whiteness is left out of the discourse. Elijah Muhammad offered a historical, psychological, and social analysis of Whiteness. He began by discussing the origin of the "White man."

The White man, according to his teachings, is the result of a Black man named Yakub (E. Muhammad, 1965). Yakub at six years old, while playing with two pieces, realized that opposites attract. This gave him the idea to produce a man that would be the opposite of the Black man. This new man would be a kind of man—*mankind*—not exactly like the original. Yakub went to work studying genetics and at the age of eighteen completed his doctoral studies.

Elijah Muhammad (1993b) wrote, "This man Yakub discovered in the germ of the black man, that he had two people in him, and had learned that this second germ could produce a powerful people that would be able to rule that which they came from" (p. 6). Yakub was not only a scientist but also a teacher who attracted followers to his message of "luxury and the making of slaves of others" (E. Muhammad, 1965, p. 113). The authorities were fearful that he would gain enough followers to take over the holy city of Mecca.

After he was arrested for his teachings, an agreement was reached between him and the authorities. He would take his followers and go to the island of Patmos or Pelan, where he would be given twenty years of supplies to develop his country. While on the island with his 59,999 followers, he used an organizational framework that would allow his ideas to continue without his physical presence. In the study of organizational theory, one will find that it mimics Yakub's strategy to make a White man.

From his study of the Black and Brown germ, he began grafting the germ to its last state. It took him six hundred years to produce a White man. Using laborers who consisted of doctors, nurses, ministers, and cremators, they would kill the Black baby and would inform the mother that the baby was an angel baby that went to heaven. When the Brown baby was born, they would marry the lighter with the lighter. In the first two hundred years, they produced the Brown man, in the next two hundred years the Yellow man, and in the sixth hundredth year the White man.

The nature in the White man would be to kill the aboriginal people. Regarding the evil tendency in the White man to destroy aboriginal people, Elijah Muhammad (1965) wrote,

> By teaching nurses to kill the black baby and save the brown baby, so as to graft the white out of it; by lying to the black mother of the baby, this lie was born into the very nature of the white baby; and, murder for the black people also born in them—or made by nature a liar and murderer. (p. 116)

Elijah Muhammad (1993b) declared the skin color of Whiteness is not a problem and that people of different colors can live alongside each other peacefully. He argued that it is the characteristics of people that are of most importance. Whiteness is not a skin color per se but an ideology that gave birth to White supremacy. When he said the White man is the devil, he was referring to the grafting process. He taught that anytime we graft from the original, we get devil (E. Muhammad, 1993b).

European rule brought out the imperfection in the human being. Thus, the Western-centric world is based on materialism. For example, the earth produces food freely, but in the White world, he steals the land and gains control of the food source. He then uses paper (money) to create power for himself. The consumer gives the landowner a dollar in return for something that the earth produces freely.

In schools, the Eurocentric philosophy of education is to prepare the masses for work and participation in his social order (Spring, 2011). Thus, people spend eight hours a day at work and school. Families rarely spend quality time with each other except on holidays that the ruling group sanctions. The teaching methods and assessments are also forms of racism and White supremacy (Pitre et al., 2021).

When Elijah Muhammad articulated the history of Whites first originating from the mind of a Black scientist to their time in the caves of Europe, he was disrupting White supremacy in very profound ways. For example, he taught that *Europe* meant "tied in" or "roped in" to keep Whites away from the aboriginal people (E. Muhammad, 1965). He then disclosed how the dog became important to the cave dwellers (Europeans), who would later become transformed by the literature they received from Moses. The knowledge that Moses shared raised the former cave dwellers into prominence.

Lastly, according to Elijah Muhammad, the White man's world would last six thousand years. The coming of Master Fard Muhammad meant the end of the White man's world. In his book *The Fall of America*, Elijah Muhammad (1973) described all the current events that were taking place in 2021. He talked about police killing Black people in the streets of America's cities, the chemical bacteriologists who were making chemicals to kill the masses, and the change of weather patterns.

The Fall of America contains a chapter that details the fall and destruction of America's educational system. The fall of America's educational system meant the destruction of White rule as a world power. He argued that without proper education, the people would begin to live on the level of beasts, and this would lead to the destruction of their world. Under the education of the "White man," the higher human powers were put to death.

Blacks in America were placed in savage conditions, and they needed a literature that would civilize and place them back into their original selves, which is the God of the universe. Today Black popular culture artists refer to themselves as *beast* and *savage*. The architects of the music industry promote a degenerative and misogynist culture that promotes and glamorizes *nigga culture* (W. Muhammad, 2017). Nigga culture is the antithesis of a high-class civilization.

Through tricknology, the masses are trained to love the culture that produces death. Drugs, guns, and sex become tools that the adversary of God uses to guide people to a culture of death. In the Bible, Jesus declares that he comes to bring life abundantly, whereas his adversary comes to bring death. This coming of Christ is to bring knowledge that will free the people from the lower forms of life that cause them to live a savage existence.

Yakub, the maker of the White race, lived to be only 150 years old, but his organizational genius allowed his idea of making a White man to come to fruition. The people who were in the inner circle of Yakub's planning are present today through their offspring, and they are quietly working to keep their world order alive through the ruling heads of the White man's world. In the Holy Quran, God tells Satan to use his voice to lead the people astray. Is this the entertainment industry?

A deeper study of Elijah Muhammad's teachings really means that the God of the White man is a Black God. He said, "Yakub was the God of his people and he made gods out them" (E. Muhammad, 2006, p. 206). It would also mean that the two Gods at the destruction or end of the White man's world would be two Black Gods, with one of them being Satan.

The field of critical White studies is important in destroying White supremacy. Elijah Muhammad's teachings on the origin of Whiteness are key to giving birth to a world that transcends the -isms that have caused human suffering. Islam represented a path to help Whites come out of the thinking that they are better because of their phenotype.

Dorothy Fardan (2001), the first known White person to declare followership of Elijah Muhammad, stated that he offered a critique of Whiteness during a time when White scholars were conducting studies on Blacks. Brooks and Theoharis (2019), in *Whiteucation: Privilege, Power, and Prejudice in School and Society*, make many of the same points that Elijah Muhammad articulated years ago, arguing that White dominance in education hides other ways of educating.

CONCLUSION

Elijah Muhammad's teachings were a forerunner of critical pedagogy, critical race theory, and critical Whiteness studies. His powerful critique and the truths that he taught influenced an entire movement premised on social justice. Elijah Muhammad was a miracle, a wonder among us. With only a fourth-grade education, he brought a wellspring of knowledge that is impacting all spheres of existence.

The humble Elijah Muhammad (1967) said of himself, "I was blind, deaf and dumb as anyone else of my people" (p. 4). Found in a drunken state, this little man from the sharecropping fields of Georgia grew to become a leading scientist and continues to impact the world in profound ways. At the time he was teaching these profound truths, he was attacked by those seeking to maintain dominance over Blacks in America. And because he offered a critique of the social order that went beyond the scope of Whiteness, he was labeled a hate teacher.

In the twenty-first century, his teachings are cloaked in theoretical frameworks such as critical pedagogy, critical race theory, and critical Whiteness studies. Unfortunately, these critical education scholars do not mention his name, and they continue to follow the mainstream discourse of crediting his popular pupil, Malcolm X, who they can conveniently say left behind the racist teachings of Elijah Muhammad. Elijah Muhammad offered a completely new education, one that would become the foundation of a new world. He connected, for example, the study of astronomy to the Black man, articulating how the universe came into existence. In most colleges and universities, there is no discussion of the Black man and the origins of planets and the life that exists on those planets. It is one of the reasons that he did not use the term "African" to identify Black people. For him, Black was universal, and Black people could be found on other planets like Mars.

The teachings of Elijah Muhammad are fueling the technological advances that we are experiencing today. Scientists from all over the globe are using ideas that he disclosed, and his teachings continue to stretch the human imagination.

Chapter Five

Soul Crafting

The purpose of education for Elijah Muhammad was vastly different from the Western-centric ideology that governs educational policies and practices. In contrast to human capitalist economics, which sees education as preparation for work, Elijah Muhammad's ideas went beyond work skills.

He believed education should not only prepare students for work but also be the engine for stimulating ideas that would lead one to become a job producer (E. Muhammad, 1965, 1974). Moreover, he believed proper education would raise Blacks from the mental death they experienced under oppressive rule. Malcolm X pointed out that Blacks in America were scientifically made into a people who were mentally dead—Negro (Pitre, 2019).

For Elijah Muhammad (1974), education was soul stirring, giving birth to the creative mind. His mission was to awaken Blacks to their inner powers, growing them beyond the materialism of the Western-centric world (E. Muhammad, 1965). By way of European dominance, Blacks in America were dead to the reality of self, unaware that their collective plight was connected to the appearance of God to establish justice in the earth (Cone, 2010; Muhammad, 1965). Even more importantly, they were unaware that God had visited America to set them free.

The first step in their freedom was to be introduced to a body of knowledge that would stir their appetite for knowledge. Once the teacher within was awakened, they would be on a path that led to higher degrees of consciousness. Elijah Muhammad insisted that Blacks in America had to be reeducated (Pitre, 2021c). Education would be the light that would draw out of Blacks their gifts and talents. Over his many years of teaching, Elijah Muhammad taught Blacks from all walks of life, and his influence brought out Black genius, which led to the Black consciousness movement.

Today the gifts and talents of Blacks are on full display in every field and endeavor. The descendants of former slaves form the soul of America, giving creativity to folk songs like "The Star-Spangled Banner," to the basketball court where Black men fly, to gospel preachers who mesmerize their audiences, and to others whose souls give life to the world.

Many of these Black geniuses had to survive schools that were talent killers whose primary focus was on test scores. Occasionally, they ran into teachers and others who touched their souls. The reach of the Nation of Islam is not confined to those who are considered Muslims; it extends into the diversity of the human family.

The teachings of Elijah Muhammad developed the leadership capacity within Black people. Muhammad Ali became one of the first Black sports figures to mesmerize White audiences with his eloquence and knowledge. Under the tutelage of Elijah Muhammad, leadership begins with the discovery of one's unique gifts and talents—knowledge of self. The manifestation of this gift causes one to become influential, a leader.

Elijah Muhammad's soul crafting produced a community of servant leaders. His followers experienced a new form of education that gave them purpose for living. Along the lines of purposefulness, as a student of the Holy Quran and Bible, Elijah Muhammad believed that human beings were created for a purpose: to discover the uniqueness of their being. Human beings are an expression of God.

Portrayed by the media as a hate teacher and a reverse racist, Elijah Muhammad represented a paradigm shift in the world of education. Whereas the education of Black people in the United States was designed to make them submissive to dominant rule, Elijah Muhammad prepared his students to challenge these untruths with actual facts.

Elijah Muhammad was a forerunner of African-centered and multicultural education. The knowledge he disclosed brought Blacks out of bowels of American life that formed a culture that deadened their spiritual power. In the newly formed culture, his followers learned to pray five times a day, changed their eating habits, threw away dehumanizing vocabulary, and discarded garments that exposed their physical beauty.

He eliminated hatred and division that led to fratricide, and he pointed out the role of Europeans in producing a death culture among Blacks. This placed him in direct opposition to those ruling the society.

Throughout the Black sojourn, those ruling the country were determined to control the body of knowledge that Blacks would receive (Watkins, 2001)—from the era of slavery, when it was a crime for Blacks to read, to contemporary times, when politicians, think tanks, and the superrich control the education of Blacks (Spring, 2011, 2016).

Today, it could be argued that education has been weaponized against Black and Brown students to deter them from achieving freedom, justice, and equality. Through high-stakes tests that are designed to stifle creativity, students are told they are failures because they do not do well on prepackaged material that is designed to kill their interest in knowing (Ladson-Billings, 2021). Education in the interest of the oppressor class aligns with what Paulo Freire (2018) called domestication.

Teachers unconsciously become major catalysts in the domestication of students. The schooling process leads educators to become laborers who play a major role in maintaining these systems of education (Illich, 1971) The model that is used to maintain these systems is based on organizational strategies like those that Elijah Muhammad (1993b) described in the origin of the *White man*. Through hegemony, the educational system prepares educators to accept policies and practices that are oppressive (McLaren, 2015).

Trained in educator-preparation programs that are connected to state departments, the majority of future educators are not exposed to critical educational theory and as a result are kept unaware of how education can serve as a tool to domesticate or liberate people. Moreover, numerous teacher-education programs are steeped in Eurocentric orientations (Picower & Kohli, 2017).

As a result, some teachers might unknowingly be complicit in racist policies and practices (King, 2015). In part, educator-preparation programs do not offer models of spiritual teachers. By exposing educators to spiritual teachers, they would begin to envision education as more than job preparation and perhaps see it as *soul crafting*.

Elijah Muhammad offered a model of education that was deeply spiritual. This chapter explores the spiritual component of his teachings in the context of education, identifying this as soul crafting. Cornel West said that soul crafting

> is the formation of attention that gets us to attend to the things that matter, not the things on the surface. It's the cultivation of thinking critically for yourself so you're willing to speak in such a way that you exercise what Socrates called parrhesia, which is clear speech, frank speech, fearless speech, unintimidated speech, speech that flows from your soul not to show that you're clever and smart, but to show that you're courageous and wise. (Cunningham, 2018)

Students in the Nation of Islam, because of their critical thinking and frank speech, were loved and hated. Elijah Muhammad's love for Black people compelled him to teach profound truths at the risk of his own life. Today his image is largely distorted because his program of reeducation disrupts spiritual wickedness in high places that continues to enslave people. Soul crafting for Elijah Muhammad went beyond the Greek definition to discovering one's inner powers—discovery of self. It is rooted in the teachings and lived experiences of prophets and messengers.

This chapter examines Elijah Muhammad's practice of soul crafting through the lens of his most noted pupils. It explores the goals of education beyond materialism, and it takes a spiritual tone using theology to center educational discourse. Elijah Muhammad epitomized the role of a teacher. Soul crafting was at the core of his personal development from his life experiences in the South with a speech impediment to his heavy drinking in Detroit, Michigan, where he met Mr. Fard, who deposited so much knowledge into him that it completely changed him.

The sharecropper's son through reeducation became the engine behind a whole new consciousness that shook up the ideological foundations that supported White rule throughout the world (Conyers, 2007). His students, with little to no formal education, became master teachers. The most noted of these students were Minister Malcolm X, Imam Warith D. Mohammed, Minister Muhammad Ali, and Minister Louis Farrakhan.

THE PUPILS

The section that follows highlights the lives four well-known pupils of Elijah Muhammad. In the context of education, we see a critical Black pedagogy emerging from his students. Critical Black pedagogy entails four major tenets: (1) an African-centered perspective, (2) multicultural education, (3) critical pedagogy, and (4) African American spirituality. The pupils of Elijah Muhammad would be described in the language of educational theorists as critical pedagogues.

These four noted students of Elijah Muhammad experienced transformations in their personal lives. Minister Malcolm X, Minister Muhammad Ali, and Minister Louis Farrakhan did not have college degrees; nor were they on a trajectory that would have caused them to become warriors for equal justice. Imam Warith D. Mohammed was the exception among the group because he was reared in an Islamic home environment.

Minister Malcolm was an eighth-grade dropout who was serving a prison sentence when he heard the teachings of Elijah Muhammad. Muhammad Ali was Cassius Clay, a boxer who was in the sporting world. Ali graduated nearly last in his class and noted that he was practically illiterate. He was on the boxing circuit when he was introduced to the teachings of Elijah Muhammad.

Louis Farrakhan, while having a more advanced elementary education because he attended the famed Boston Latin School for a period, was a college dropout and calypso singer. Louis Farrakhan was told about the teachings of Elijah Muhammad while performing at a night club. None of these men could have imagined they would become world leaders who would challenge the ruling powers. Moreover, their voices continue to ring out loud.

The exception of the group was Imam Warith D. Mohammed, also known as Wallace D. Muhammad, who was the son of Elijah Muhammad. Growing up in an Islamic home, Imam Mohammed would be responsible for developing the pathway to Al-Islam. He was a student at the University of Islam, where he studied Orthodox Islam from one of the teachers in the school. The imam developed an Islamic teaching that originated with his father's teachings.

The teachings of Elijah Muhammad produced leaders. Maxwell (1998), speaking about the attributes of great leaders, says they know about the law of reproduction, which is to produce other leaders. The ability to produce other leaders was one of the hallmarks of Elijah Muhammad's legacy. At the core of Elijah Muhammad's leadership legacy was the practice of servant leadership.

The students of Elijah Muhammad were referred to as ministers, which etymologically means "servant." And they were expected to serve the needs of the downtrodden, the oppressed, the Blacks who were at the bottom of the social order. Robert Greenleaf (n.d.) described servant leadership as beginning "with the natural feeling that one wants to serve, to serve first. Then conscious choice brings one to aspire to lead. The person is sharply different from one who is leader first, perhaps of the need to assuage of an unusual power drive or to acquire material possessions" (p. 27).

The students of Elijah Muhammad were not cognizant they were being prepared for leadership. They were first consumed with gaining knowledge, and this created a desire in them to share this knowledge with the downtrodden Blacks in society. They were concerned with ensuring the needs of Black people were being met and believed the Nation of Islam was the vehicle toward true freedom. Greenleaf (n.d.) posited that the test of leadership is to ensure that those under one's leadership "become healthier, wiser, freer, and more autonomous" (p. 27).

At the core of their willingness to serve was the radical love they had for Black people. This radical love was expressed by the founder of the Nation of Islam, Master Fard Muhammad, who studied for twenty years the English language in order to relay a message to Blacks in America.

In total, he studied for forty-two years what he intended to teach Blacks in America and as a result was jailed on more than one occasion for teaching freedom, justice, equality, and independence. When Elijah Muhammad became the *Messenger* of Allah, he met the same fate of persecution and death threats. As a child he grew up with a deep love for Black people after having experienced lynchings and other sufferings in the South. It was his love for Black people that caused him to make his word bond with his teacher that he would die in the pursuit of liberating Black people. This is the radical love that he awakened in his students and those who were his true followers.

Minister Malcolm X

Malcolm Little was born on May 19, 1925, in Omaha, Nebraska, to Earl and Louise Little. He was the fourth of seven children. His parents were members of Marcus Garvey's Universal Negro Improvement Association (Marable, 2011). His father was a preacher in the area whose stance against racism angered the local Whites, and in 1926 the Littles moved to Lansing, Michigan.

Earl Little, as follower of Marcus Garvey, may have angered local Whites in Lansing as well. He had an accident on a railroad track and later died at the hospital. While the official cause of death was reported as an accident, his wife believed otherwise. Malcolm was six years old at the time of his father's death.

The untimely death of his father forced his mother to become the main provider for the family. His mother would develop a relationship with a man by whom she would later become pregnant. The man eventually left her, leaving no trace as to his whereabouts (Haley, 1965; Marable, 2013). The tremendous stress of losing two companions caused her to suffer a nervous breakdown. As a result, Malcolm and his siblings were placed in various foster homes.

In describing one of those foster home settings, Malcolm said he felt he didn't fit in well with the family he was assigned to live with (Haley, 1965). In school, he exhibited leadership acumen by becoming president of his class despite being in a predominantly White school (Haley, 1965).

One of Malcolm's experiences in the school caused him to lose hope. He would later turn to the streets, where his leadership acumen was used for negative purposes. Malcolm's downward trajectory occurred when his teacher found him alone and took advantage of the opportunity to perhaps let him know his place in the school. Probably angered by the fact that a majority-White student body selected Malcolm as the class president, the teacher skillfully asked Malcolm, "What do you plan to do when you grow up?" Malcolm replied that he wanted to be a lawyer, to which his teacher responded,

Malcolm, one of life's first needs is for us to be realistic. Don't misunderstand me, now. We all here like you, you know that. But you've got to be realistic about being a nigger. A lawyer—that's no realistic goal for a nigger. You need to think about something you can be. You're good with your hands—making things. Everybody admires your carpentry shop work. Why don't you plan on carpentry? People like you as a person—you'd get all kinds of work. (Haley, 1965, p. 421)

Malcolm said this experience caused him to turn on the inside, and it made him lose interest in school. The teacher had effectively planted the seed that would send Malcolm to a life of crime. The experience that Malcolm had with this teacher is not uncommon in schools today. Black boys are silenced in schools, and they never discover their voices. Like Malcolm, they encounter teachers who make suggestions that turn Black students away from learning. They often have low expectations for Black students and perceive them to be like the images they have seen on television.

Nevertheless, Malcolm eventually quit school and found himself in a life of crime, which included drug dealing, the prostitution of women, the use of drugs, and larceny. Malcolm was on death row in the streets, and his arrest for larceny was a blessing in disguise.

While in prison, he was introduced to the teachings of Elijah Muhammad. These teachings touched the soul of Malcolm, causing him to become an avid reader. Moreover, he became an exceptional student of Elijah Muhammad's teachings. Perhaps the most compelling narrative of Malcolm's experience in prison was the apparition of a light-skinned man sitting on his bed in a jail cell:

I suddenly, with a start, became aware of a man sitting beside me in my chair. He had on a dark suit. I remember. I could see him as plainly as I see anyone I look at. He wasn't black, and he wasn't white. He was light-browned skin, an Asiatic cast of countenance, and had oily hair. (Haley, 1965, p. 215).

After he was released from prison, during a visit to the home of Elijah Muhammad, he noticed a picture of Master Fard Muhammad, noting this that looked like the man whose apparition appeared in his jail cell. He wrote,

It's impossible to dream, or see, or to have a vision of someone whom you have never seen before—and to see him exactly as he is. To see someone, and to see him exactly as he looks, is to have a pre-vision. I would later come to believe that my pre-vision was of Master W. D. Fard, the Messiah, the one Elijah Muhammad said had appointed him—Elijah Muhammad—as His Last Messenger to the Black people of North America (Haley, 1965, pp. 217–218).

This experience with Master Fard Muhammad has been overlooked by scholars. In part, Eurocentric education does not prepare one to understand spiritual matters. The encounter that Malcolm had with Master Fard Muhammad causes this author to believe that he was destined to become a star in the Nation of Islam. Malcolm's life experiences were perhaps intended to demonstrate the power of Elijah Muhammad's teaching to resurrect the dead.

Elijah Muhammad loved Malcolm like a son and taught him like no other minister in the Nation of Islam. He found in Malcolm a person in which he could deposit supreme wisdom (Haley, 1965). This caused Malcolm to excel in the ministry class. After he had served as a minister for several years, Elijah Muhammad appointed Malcolm as his national spokesperson in 1963, and a star was born. Malcolm shined bright in articulating the knowledge he received from Elijah Muhammad. Malcolm's articulation of this knowledge caused Blacks in America to become proud of their Blackness, and this gave rise to the Black Power movement.

Through the acquisition of knowledge, Malcolm was no longer Little but X, traveling on a path that gave him purpose. The early childhood talent that had been put to sleep by his grade-school teacher was awakened after being watered by Elijah Muhammad's teachings. As a master teacher, Elijah Muhammad gave Malcolm a platform for his brilliance to shine, and this led him to become known worldwide.

Malcolm lectured at major universities and appeared on national broadcasts, where he articulated what is now known as critical race theory and Whiteness studies. One of those lectures was at Boston University's School of Theology (Lincoln, 1960). Biographers writing about Malcolm X forget to mention there would be no Malcolm were it not for the educational program of Elijah Muhammad.

Elijah Muhammad transformed the life of Malcolm X, who had only an eighth-grade education, by providing him with the knowledge of self. Farrakhan (1993) wrote that it was the knowledge of self that caused Malcolm X to win debates against Ivy League students.

Malcolm's influence was profound and inspired the formation of Black studies programs in universities. The leading architects of Black studies were influenced by Malcolm X (Karenga, 2002). In Black studies programs, there is an array of courses that are offshoots of Elijah Muhammad's teachings (Norment, 2019).

Elijah Muhammad's teachings covered every aspect of Black life. The early founders of Black studies, while marveling at the words spoken by Malcolm, didn't necessarily take a deep study of Elijah Muhammad's teachings. Farrakhan, speaking to the relationship between Elijah Muhammad and Malcolm X, pointed out that the two had reached an agreement. The agreement was that Malcolm would be placed out front, and Elijah Muhammad would provide him with the words to convey to people (Ekiye, 2013). Farrakhan goes on to say that Malcolm was sharing what he got directly from Elijah Muhammad.

Elijah Muhammad sent Malcolm to other countries. While on these visits, the idea of Black struggle across the globe became apparent to him. In these travels, Malcolm interacted with African leaders such as Pio Gama Pinto, and the two exchanged ideas about Black liberation (Owino, 2019). Dick Gregory (2016), speaking about the assassination of Malcolm, made the observation that Pinto was assassinated three days after Malcolm on February 24, 1965, and he contended the death of both men was orchestrated by the Central Intelligence Agency.

Malcolm's influence was wide, but his jewel was influencing those who would play an important role in the establishment of Black studies. As a discipline, Black studies addresses the experiences of Black people across the globe, and inherent in it are the themes of Black liberation and self-determination (Karenga, 2002; Norment, 2019). Despite the formation of Black studies, the teachings of Elijah Muhammad far outstretched many of the intellectuals.

Whereas they may have used an African-centered perspective in their particular areas of study, Elijah Muhammad started with the origin of all life in the universe: the Black man as the original man, the God of the universe. Thus, all of the disciplines began with what the Black man created. It was terrifying to Whites to learn that the God of their creation was a Black man. Elijah Muhammad was to Malcolm what Master Fard Muhammad was to him: a teacher who touched his soul.

When Malcolm X left the building where the Nation of Islam held its meetings, he was still taken over by the teachings of Elijah Muhammad. In a speech on history, after leaving the Nation of Islam, he said a scientist mentioned that when you see a red and blue star appearing in the sky, it represents universal change (Pitre, 2019). The scientist that he is referring to is Elijah Muhammad. With his brilliant articulation of Black studies, many of the youth who were influenced by Malcolm would later become academicians. And they would even declare they were the children of Malcolm (Watkins, 2001). Here are some of the major highlights from speeches by Malcolm X, who was later given the name Malik El Hajj Shabazz:

> When you deal with the past, you are dealing with history, you are actually dealing with the origin of a thing. (Shabazz, 1967, p. 4)

> Just as a tree without roots is dead, a people without history or cultural roots becomes a dead people. (Shabazz, 1967, p. 16)

> But the Black man by nature is a builder, he is scientific by nature, he's mathematical by nature. (Shabazz, 1967, p. 22)

Malcolm, with only an eighth-grade education, was set ablaze by the teachings of Elijah Muhammad. Fueled by a knowledge that touched his soul, Malcolm experienced a metamorphosis; leaving behind a life of crime that had him aimlessly wandering, he became a man with purpose. In Malcolm, we see the power of critical Black pedagogy.

Imam Warith D. Mohammed

Imam Wallace D. Muhammad, born on October 30, 1933, was the seventh of eight children born to Elijah and Clara Muhammad. He was given the name Wallace D. Muhammad by the Nation of Islam's founder. With regard to Wallace's name, Master Fard Muhammad told Elijah that he would be a great one and should have the name Wallace D. Muhammad (Essien-Udom, 1962).

Wallace attended Muhammad University of Islam and was taught by a Muslim teacher named Jamil Diab. Jamil Diab taught the students Arabic and exposed Wallace to the orthodox teachings of Islam (Rashad, 2019). Over time, the young Wallace would begin to question his father's teachings.

It is important to note that Wallace was apart from his father for several years due to persecutions. For example, the departure of Master Fard Muhammad caused friction in the Nation of Islam, which resulted in Elijah Muhammad fleeing to the East Coast, and this led to his subsequent arrest in 1942. Wallace was apart from his father for around fourteen years.

Like his father, Wallace was sent to prison, in his case in 1960 for refusing military induction. On his release from prison, his questioning of God coming in a human form, but even more so of the divinity of Master Fard Muhammad, became more pronounced (Rashad, 2019). On at least three occasions, he was excommunicated from the Nation of Islam for teaching things that were contrary to the Nation of Islam's teachings.

On one occasion, he was on the verge of being excommunicated when his father called a meeting that brought together Wallace and those who were accusing him of altering the teachings. During this meeting, to the surprise of everyone, his father suggested they listen to the audio tape.

Shocked by the fact that his father did not hear the tape prior to the meeting, the group was astonished when Elijah Muhammad clapped and praised his son's presentation. This inspired the imam to believe his father even envisioned a new Islam that would embrace human diversity (RemembranceOfAllah, 1992/2012).

Despite grappling with aspects of his father's teachings, Wallace was a student of those teachings. The imam was a deconstructionist of his father's teachings, looking for inconsistencies with orthodox Islam. In his deconstruction, he was looking for ways to expand and make new the teachings of Elijah Muhammad. He believed the changing attitudes in America would warrant a more traditional Islam but yet something new.

The imam envisioned a new school of Islamic thought coming from America, inclusive of the diversity of racial and ethnic groups in the country.

After the death of Elijah Muhammad, Wallace assumed leadership of the Nation of Islam and moved the organization toward orthodox Islam. While many were critical of these changes, it could be argued that they were necessary, considering the agents provocateurs who were inside the organization.

It is likely many of these agents remained inside the new organization, but changing the focus caused their attacks to subside. The new changes also caused deep reflection in Minister Louis Farrakhan, which made manifest his deep love for Elijah Muhammad. This allowed him to rebuild the Nation of Islam without the interference of Nation of Islam officials.

The imam wrote several articles that demonstrated profound knowledge that bridged gaps between Christianity, Islam, and the Nation of Islam's teachings. The imam placed the Prophet Muhammad in an educational context, writing, "The perfect man and the complete man and this Prophet is a teacher—he's an educator and the miracle is that he himself was not educated" (Mohammed, 2015, p. 10).

Speaking on the condition of Blacks in America, he saw their problems in a spiritual context. While Black leaders were asking for more jobs and civil rights, the imam cogently articulated a path toward liberation:

> How to liberate people? This is the way you liberate them! He releases them from the heavy burdens and from the yokes. What are the yokes? Sin! Immorality! Vulgar behavior! Don't you know that's what got us enslaved? Why don't we have the strength and the dignity of other communities? It's because we have given ourselves to this kind of deterioration and our leaders won't stand up and say that's wrong. This is part of your problem. We're going to have to have better morals among the Blacks. (Mohammed, 2015, p. 22)

Some of the powerful quotes of Imam Warith D. Mohammed include the following:

> Jesus is the Son of the divine mind and the servant of Allah's truth can exist in any color, physical body. It just so happens that Bilalians (Blacks in America) were the people who cried out longer, more continuously, more pitifully, and more sincerely than anybody else to receive the Jesus Christ.

> It is these words that form your mind and personality. You are a creation of words.

> A human being can be born again. All you have to do is to allow yourself to be fed by a new kind of word and that will make you into a new person again.

> Education deals directly with the mind.

Warith D. Mohammed was a brilliant minister and theologian who was developed from the teachings of Elijah Muhammad. He set in motion the African American pathway to Al-Islam. A brief study of his writings demonstrates his brilliance and leadership.

Muhammad Ali

Muhammad Ali, the three-time heavyweight boxing champion, is usually referred to as the greatest of all time. It was not Ali's prowess in the boxing ring that made him the greatest; it was his cry for equal justice for Blacks in America that made him more than just a boxer. Born on January 17, 1942, in Louisville, Kentucky, under the name Cassius Clay, he was drawn to boxing after his bicycle was stolen.

After telling Joe Martin, a police officer, that he wished to whip the person responsible, Martin suggested to the young Cassius that he might consider boxing. Taking the suggestion of Martin, he visited a boxing facility and was fascinated with the sport (The Famous People, n.d.). By the age of twelve, he was fully engaged in boxing, and at the age of twenty-two, he became the heavyweight champion of the world, defeating Sonny Liston.

The shout "I am the greatest!" became the trademark of Cassius Clay, but unbeknownst to the world, he was studying Islam. The cry "I am the greatest!" represented the call that Muslims declare when they say, "Allah is the greatest."

Clay, while preparing for the fight with Sonny Liston, had been under the tutelage of Captain Sam X, later known as Abdul Rahman, who had been privately tutoring Clay about the teachings of Elijah Muhammad (R. Muhammad, 2016; Zirin, 2017). And while most writers like to refer to Malcolm X as being the person who most influenced Clay, it was Elijah Muhammad through his teachings that transformed Clay, giving him the name Muhammad Ali (Zirin, 2017; R. Muhammad, 2016).

Unfortunately, most writers have not studied the teachings of Elijah Muhammad, and many of these critics are Black writers who are the epitome of what Carter G. Woodson (1999) described as miseducated because they have been taught to view the world through a Eurocentric lens (J. Muhammad, 1996). In Africana discourse, a Black person who sees the world through a Eurocentric lens is likened to an Oreo, Black on the outside and White on the inside.

In fact, American education is symbolized by an apple, which refers to the education of Native peoples, which meant they would be red on the outside but White on the inside. The education of oppressed groups involved a deculturalization process that was designed to make non-Whites tools for those who owned the country (Watkins, 2001; Spring, 2016).

When Cassius Clay officially became a member of the Nation of Islam, he had been under a reeducation process that was making him into a man. The Nation of Islam is not an organization that you can just sign up to join; its members are required to take up study. They are then required to complete exams that demonstrate a basic knowledge of the Nation's teachings.

His giving up his slave name, Cassius Clay, and accepting the name Muhammad Ali represented what Paulo Freire described as dislodging the oppressor consciousness that resides in the oppressed. Freire (2018) wrote that the oppressed have internalized the oppressor consciousness to the degree that they are afraid to seek freedom. Grounded in a universal knowledge, Ali was confident, and this made him not only a boxer but also a "man" who frustrated White interviewees because they could not defeat his arguments.

Muhammad Ali embodied soul crafting, being fearless in the face of mostly White audiences. When speaking in an interview with *Black Scholar* about going to jail because of his refusal to go to Vietnam, he poetically stated,

Hell no,
I ain't going to go
Clean out my cell
And take my tail to jail
Without bail
Because it's better there eating
Watching television fed
Than in Vietnam with your white folks dead. (History.com Editors, 2018)

It was his courageousness that cause him to place his boxing career aside to advocate for those who were living under oppressive conditions. It was this soul crafting that Ali experienced that allowed him to find a bigger purpose in life.

And while nearly every person writing about Muhammad Ali tries to discredit or distance him from the "the Most Honorable Elijah Muhammad," it was this master teacher who did the *soul crafting*, or bringing out the good, in Muhammad Ali, starting with him giving him the name Muhammad Ali on March 6, 1964 (Townsend et al., 2018).

Muhammad means "one worthy of praise and praised much," and *Ali* means "high," "elevated," or "champion." Muhammad Ali lived up to this name because he was deeply in love with his teacher. Beyond his death, he is praised and considered to be the greatest *champion* of all time.

When he threw off the name Clay, it angered many people, and for years journalists and others refused to acknowledge him as Muhammad Ali (Townsend et al., 2018). They were angered because the name Muhammad Ali represented the birthing of a human being who was critically conscious of the forces that sought to dehumanize Blacks in America.

He was now striving to become more godlike by throwing off the "slave master's name." Ironically, like the *clay* described in the Holy Quran, this Clay grew into a living spirit. The Holy Quran, in Chapter 15, verses 28–29, refers to clay: "And when thy Lord said to the angels: I am going to create a mortal of sounding clay, of black mud fashioned into shape. So when I have made him complete and breathed into him of My spirit, fall down making obeisance to him." Clay transfigured earthly chains and was made complete through his acquisition of knowledge that led him to the doing of good for the whole of humanity.

Minister Louis Farrakhan

Born on May 11, 1933, as Louis Walcott to Sarah Mae Manning, who was a Caribbean woman from St. Kitts, in the Bronx, New York, he would become a member of the Nation of Islam in 1955. The circumstances around Farrakhan's birth were unusual, as his mother attempted to abort her pregnancy on three occasions (Pitre, 2018), in part because she had been romantically involved with two men and was not sure who was the father.

Despite her struggles, his mother was committed to ensuring that he would receive an excellent education. She placed the violin in his hands and sent him to the famed Boston Latin School, where greats like Benjamin Franklin and Ralph Waldo Emmerson were former students. The lack of diversity caused him to feel out of place, and he eventually withdrew from the school.

Like Malcolm X, he also encountered racism in school when his teacher asked him what he planned to do when he grew up. He replied, "I want to become a doctor because I want to heal people." She replied, "Oh Louis, if you became a doctor my people would never come to you and your own people wouldn't trust your medical skill. But you play the violin beautifully" (J. Muhammad, 2006, p. 340).

He saw this experience as the teacher's way of motivating him toward a nonthreatening career, but nonetheless reflected on his musical talents and believed that he could serve humanity by giving them music. As a young child, he was concerned with the plight of Black people because his mother exposed the family to the writings of Marcus Garvey and W. E. B. Du Bois.

At eleven years of age, while visiting family in New York, he observed a picture on the wall (Muhammad, 2006). Inquisitive, he asked who the man was. He was told it was Marcus Garvey, a man who had come to help Black people. The young Louis was inspired and wanted to find out where he could meet Mr. Garvey, only to find out that he had passed away. This brought him to tears because he had longed to meet someone who could relieve Blacks of their suffering. As young boy, he was a member of and involved in St. Cyprians Episcopal Church. Like his soon-to-be teacher, Elijah Muhammad, Louis wondered, If God had sent a deliverer to other oppressed people, why didn't he send someone to Blacks in America? (Angelis, 1998).

During his high school years, he was a standout student athlete, excelling in track. After completing high school, he decided to go south. He wanted to experience what Blacks in the South lived under and enrolled in Winston Salem Teachers College (Person-Lynn, 1996). After two years, he left the university to take care of his girlfriend, who was pregnant. He picked up his musical career as a calypso singer and started singing at night clubs.

While performing at one of the night clubs, he was invited to attend the Nation of Islam's Savior's Day Convention (Person-Lynn, 1996). Prior to that, he had a brief encounter with Malcolm X but didn't have an interest in the Nation of Islam because of its purportedly racist teachings (Person-Lynn, 1996). Despite his reservations, he decided to attend the Nation of Islam's Savior's Day Convention in February 1955.

As he listened to Elijah Muhammad, he thought to himself, This man doesn't speak well:

I, being a student of English, and verb and subject agreement, heard him speak in a manner that a public speaker who was familiar with English wouldn't do. So, in my head I said, "Oh this man can't even talk." When I said that he looked right at me and said, Brother, I didn't get a chance to get that fine education that you got. When I got to the school the doors was closed. (J. Muhammad, 2006, p. 334)

Reading his thoughts, Elijah Muhammad looked at him in the balcony and said, "Don't pay attention to how I'm saying it. You pay attention to what I'm saying and then you take it and put it in that fine language that you know. Only try to understand what I'm saying" (J. Muhammad, 2006, p. 333). This shocked the destined-to-be minister in the Nation of Islam. After accepting the teachings of Elijah Muhammad, Louis Walcott would eventually receive the name Farrakhan.

Prior to receiving the name Farrakhan, he had to give up his promising career as a calypso singer (Muhammad, 2006). Traveling on faith and his love for Black people, he became the prized pupil of Elijah Muhammad. He has been a student of Elijah Muhammad's teachings for sixty-plus years, compared to Malcolm X, who studied for around twelve years.

He has articulated knowledge in every discipline found in the major universities. In 1995, he led nearly two million Black men to Washington, DC, to make a commitment to change their lives and communities. Today he is a standout world leader who has taken the teachings of Elijah Muhammad across the globe. The college dropout has become the source of knowledge from which millions have been watered to become human beings committed to the doing of good for the whole of humanity.

In the context of education, his work reflects concepts found in critical educational theory, and he has lectured extensively on education. Below are some of his quotes on education:

Knowledge feeds the development of human beings so that the person can grow and evolve into Divine and become one with the creator. (Farrakhan, 1993, p. 47)

He who gives the diameter of your knowledge prescribes the circumference of your activity. (Farrakhan, 1993, p. 48)

I tremble for my country when I reflect that God is just and that his justice cannot sleep forever. (Farrakhan, 2006, p. 21)

We cannot have power without proper knowledge, for it is knowledge properly exercised and implemented that gives us power. (Farrakhan, 1992)

Farrakhan is one of the last remaining voices from the Black Freedom Movement of the 1960s. His powerful messages continue to transform the lives of the millennial generation. Though he is nearly ninety years old, his popularity among the youth continues to grow despite negative media attention.

THE POWER OF LOVE

The one commonality found among the students of Elijah Muhammad is their love for Black people. They were all driven by the mission of resurrecting the dead, which refers to Blacks in America who did not have a knowledge of self or the time in which they lived. Knowledge was the key to unlocking the human potential that lay dormant in Blacks in America. This knowledge was not the knowledge prescribed in the traditional school per se but was spiritual, in the sense that it overshadowed, but also gave deeper meaning to, the subjects taught in traditional public schools.

KNOWLEDGE OF SELF

Elijah Muhammad's education program began with the knowledge of self. The idea of grounding education in discovery of the self is not new and is the basis of elite education (Gatto, 2017). When Elijah Muhammad (1965) declared the greatest of all knowledge to be knowing oneself, he was setting up an education system for Blacks that would make them world rulers. Knowledge of self-meant taking a deep study of history, but it also dealt with a spiritual component that addressed the unique purpose and role of one's existence in the universe. Elijah Muhammad taught that knowledge of self and God were intertwined.

For most people in America, their concept of God was based on a Eurocentric worldview. Through the Western construction of Christianity, this made all the significant persons in the Bible White men. Jesus and all the disciples were White men with English names. These images of divinity form the foundation for racism and White supremacy. Elijah Muhammad disrupted this belief when he disclosed that the Supreme Being, the originator of the heavens and the earth, is a Black man.

This caused him to say that a careful study of history would reveal that Blacks had civilizations that were superior to what we are currently experiencing (E. Muhammad, 1965). The Black man, according to his teachings, is the architect of the universe, and his wisdom was hidden to allow Whites to rule for six thousand years. After six thousand years, a new God would be born to supplant White rule (E. Muhammad, 1965, 1974). Elijah Muhammad's discourse was centered around race in all subject matters, and this caused him to be labeled as a racist or reverse racist (Pipes, 2000).

Depending on how "racist" is defined, the label could be correct. Racists, according to scholars of racism, have power to impose laws that negatively impact the way of life of people in a society (Diangelo, 2018; Nieto & Bode, 2018). Diangelo (2018) writes, "When a racial group's collective prejudice is backed by the power of legal authority and institutional control, it is transformed into racism, a far-reaching system that functions independently from the intentions or self-images of individual actors" (p. 20).

According to this definition, Muhammad could not be defined as a racist because he did not have the power to establish laws that could negatively impact Whites. On the other hand, Minister Farrakhan (2020) retorted that a racist could also be somebody who is committed to the study and advancement of their race. In this definition, one might conclude that Elijah Muhammad was a racist.

Undergirding the idea of race, Elijah Muhammad declared that Blacks did not belong to a race. Race has a beginning and ending point. He taught that the Black man does not have a beginning or end and is the origin from which races come to exist (E. Muhammad, 1974, 1993, 2006). However, throughout his teachings, he believed in treating all people regardless of race with dignity, respect, and justice. His goal was to grow his students into seeing the oneness of humanity, thus making them teachers of the whole of humanity.

Elijah Muhammad's teachings addressed the issue of race because it permeated every aspect of American society (Delgado & Stefancic, 2017). While critical race theorists have asserted that race and racism are part of everyday American life, it was Elijah Muhammad who connected race to all fields of study (Abdullah, 2016).

The goal of education for Elijah Muhammad was to restore Blacks to greatness, which meant oneness with the creator. His teachings made people conscious of the underlying ideology that led to White rule. When he critiqued the educational system, he pointed out that it would not be used in the new world (E. Muhammad, 1974).

Many of his students, after becoming conscious of the greatness of Black people and knowledgeable about how society was constructed to support White supremacy, were then ready to take on advanced studies. These advanced studies led them to become students of the Holy Quran. As they pored over the depth of the words emanating from the Prophet Muhammad, they began to understand how the Holy Quran confirmed the Bible.

Elijah Muhammad's students could be classified as Chrislamists because they understood the practices or ways of life of the prophets and messengers as told in diverse scriptures. Guided by both the Bible and the Holy Quran, they began to gain a better understanding of the restrictive laws of the Nation of Islam. These restrictive laws included abstinence from fornication, tobacco, alcohol or intoxicating drinks, gambling, and filthy language, among many other restrictions.

These restrictive laws were punctuated with the necessity of praying five time per day and striving to eat one meal a day. Over time, the followers of these restrictive laws began to change their outer appearance. This change of the physical appearance reflected new thoughts and ideas that were taking place internally: "As you notice, the effect of thoughts or your thinking at times has such a deep effect on the brain that it affects the surface of your face, skin, and body" (E. Muhammad, 1974, p. 124).

Study in the Nation of Islam was like an act of prayer, because it became personal and was treasured, bringing peace and contentment of mind (Pinar, 2005). Elijah Muhammad, through his articulation of supreme wisdom, sparked in his students the desire to learn, which was part of the resurrection process that brought to life the teacher within.

This teacher within caused some students in the Nation of Islam to be guided by the supreme guide. Through reading the Holy Quran, some of these students could hear the voice of God speaking to them (T. Muhammad, 2021b). This gave them a certain peace and joy. They could then walk among those ruling the society, knowing they had a knowledge that was superior. And without degrees from White institutions, they baffled the minds of the most intellectual persons in the society.

The knowledge of self made every subject relevant to his well-learned students. Minister Farrakhan (1993) pointed out that the subjects are not external and that students in the Nation of Islam are taught "I am Biology," "I am Mathematics," and "I am History." It was not only the knowledge that Elijah Muhammad espoused that transformed the lives of his students but also his love for people that made him an extraordinary teacher.

When he saw Black people in the streets engaged in self-destructive behavior, he yearned to teach them. Unlike public schools, where teachers might have low expectations of Black students, he knew that they were sleeping gods. This led him to say that every time you see a Black man, you are looking at God (E. Muhammad, 2019).

In the 1970s, before his death, he was setting up a teachers' college in Sedalia, North Carolina. His idea to do this is an example of his divine wisdom. North Carolina can be likened to a Mecca of Black education because it boasts more historically Black colleges and universities than any other state.

Elijah Muhammad recognized the need for a teachers' college to prepare educators for Black students. Ladson-Billings (2021) wrote that one of the flaws of teacher-preparation programs is that they are not intentional in preparing teachers who can educate Black students. Elijah Muhammad understood that teachers needed to be philosophically oriented in a critical Black consciousness.

Teachers with a critical Black consciousness are needed now more than ever. In *Black Power*, Kwame Toure and Charles Hamilton (1992) highlighted a study of Black teachers, noting that while having tremendous potential to transform Black lives, they were beholden to the White power structure. The authors went on to say that the same practices used to colonize African countries were at work in America through the selection of Black leaders who were willing to be puppets of the White power structure.

In public school systems that are predominantly made up of Black and Brown students, the superintendent positions are being filled with non-Whites. While on the surface it appears that this means progress, it could also be a skillful way of making non-Whites the face of racist school policies. Even more disturbing are the teachers who are skillfully making Black students hate school. Examples of this are when Black boys are not called on when their hands are raised or when they have to try twice as hard to get teachers' attention (Nieto & Bode, 2018).

And once these teachers have frustrated Black students, and their frustration causes them to respond, they are sent to the office for punishment by the Black principal. Teachers are muting Black boys in school while at the same time displaying a bond with White students.

White males are elevated to leadership roles in the school, and Black boys are silenced or made invisible. This led Elijah Muhammad to argue that Black children needed to be in separate schools until the age of sixteen to give Black people a chance to shape their children—in other words, to build their identities and root them in the knowledge of self (E. Muhammad, 1965).

Elijah Muhammad pointed out that the job of the teacher was to teach civilization, which meant culture and refinement. The whole mission of Elijah Muhammad was education. It was spiritual and was called the resurrection of the dead. Once Black students were raised from the dead, ideas would begin to flow from them.

These ideas would catapult them into leadership. Leadership is the discovery of the unique gift that the creator has bestowed upon or deposited in the human being. Once this gift is discovered and actualized, it influences people, causing them to gravitate toward it. The person who has actualized their gift is on the path to leadership.

The study of education could begin with the sperm. The sperm is a mixture of water and vegetation. It is useless until it is placed in the right environment. Minister Farrakhan pointed out that there is intelligence in the head of the sperm. This intelligence causes the sperm to swim to the egg against the odds; once there, it forms a clot, and while in triple darkness, the head calls the other body parts into existence. Farrakhan pointed out that God works in the darkness to evolve the clot into an embryo and then the birthing of a human being, complete yet incomplete (Pitre, 2018).

From a humble beginning of water and vegetation, the human being is on a journey to discover the self. This journey of self-discovery is supported by knowledge, and it is knowledge that leads to being one with the creator. For Elijah Muhammad, the woman was the centerpiece of civilization and the cornerstone of education.

He pointed out that the woman is the first teacher. She is the mother who, by nature, provides physical and spiritual substance needed for one to survive (E. Muhammad, 1965). The woman in the Nation of Islam needed to be highly educated because it was through her that the civilization would be advanced.

Elijah Muhammad (1965) pointed out that when you teach a man, you are teaching an individual, but when you teach a woman, you are teaching a nation. In the Nation of Islam, the woman is treasured and is sacred. In the Nation of Islam's teachings, harming a woman is one of the acts that can justify taking a human life.

Likewise, the classroom should represent the mother. It should be a place filled with love and commitment for the betterment of students. Like the womb of the mother, the classroom gives birth to ideas generated from students. Instead of testing for knowledge, the reimagined classroom brings out creativity. Viewed in this way, the woman is the cornerstone of society, and her education produces a nation of gods.

CONCLUSION

Education in the Nation of Islam is a spiritual undertaking. Elijah Muhammad (1965) declared, "The duty of the civilized man is to teach civilization to the uncivilized—the arts and sciences of civilized people and countries of advanced civilization. . . . His message teaches spiritual civilization, which is important to the success of a nation and society" (p. 44).

The spiritual component provides students with a deeper understanding of the purpose of studying the subjects. Today, concepts such as culturally relevant pedagogy and culturally sustaining pedagogy have similarities to the spiritual components found in Elijah Muhammad's teachings.

One aspect of culturally relevant pedagogy is to use the students' cultural experiences as a bridge to connect with academic content

(Ladson-Billings, 1995). Elijah Muhammad's teaching deconstructed the culture that Blacks in America found themselves living under, and he taught them how their current way of life was engineered by those ruling society. The socially engineered culture was a form of hegemony that caused Blacks to contribute to their own demise. Scholars use the term "hegemony," but Elijah Muhammad (1993c) called it "tricknology."

Through historical study, the students of Elijah Muhammad began to see how they were living a life that was foreign to their original selves. This foreign life was identified as a bestial life or savage way of existing. As a result of these teachings, his students became conscious of how public schools were designed to keep them in servitude:

> Certainly, the so-called Negroes are being schooled, but is this education the equal of that of their slave-masters? No; the so-called Negroes are still begging for equal education. After blinding them to the knowledge of self and their own kind for 400 years, the slave-masters refuse to civilize the so-called Negroes into the knowledge of themselves of which they were robbed. The slave-masters also persecute and hinder anyone who tries to perform this most rightful duty. (E. Muhammad, 1965, pp. 44–45)

In the above quote, Elijah Muhammad addressed educational philosophy and questions of curriculum. Philosophically, he believed the education of Blacks in America should prepare them for building an independent nation. He was an Afro-pessimist and critical race forerunner, believing that Blacks would never get equal justice in US society:

> We were brought here not to be made Americans or American citizens but rather to be slaves or servants for the true American citizens, whites who originally came from Europe. We, descendants of the Asiatic nation from the continent of Africa after 100 years of so-called freedom, cannot claim by the law of justice to be Americans or American citizens. Nor can we expect anything like equal justice under the law of true American courts. (E. Muhammad, 1965, p. 184)

Regarding the curriculum, he believed that those ruling society would never allow the majority of its schools to teach Blacks in America the knowledge of self. At best, the closest that they have gotten to his teachings being implemented in public schools and universities is in the Black studies programs that emerged in colleges and universities in the 1960s.

One of the leading architects of Black studies is Maulana Karenga (2007), who is knowledgeable of the teachings of Elijah Muhammad, which perhaps played a role in shaping many of his ideas around Kawaida. Karenga created Kwanzaa, and a careful reading of his Kawaida theory, along with the seven principles of Nguzo Saba, reveals many similarities to the teachings of Elijah Muhammad.

Molefi Asante (1991), the author of the Afrocentric idea in education, throughout his many writings has mentioned Elijah Muhammad's contributions to the study of Black people. And while Black studies is in part a product of Elijah Muhammad's teachings, he is virtually absent in the Black studies discourse; as a result, the power of Black studies has not maximized its true potential. Moreover, Black studies programs are not offered at most historically Black colleges and universities.

In public schools, the foundational philosophy is based on not producing gods but, to the contrary, stifling the creative mind. And when teachers and administrators reflect a Black consciousness, they are very likely to be persecuted (Pitre, 2011). Elijah Muhammad (1965) eloquently said it was important for Blacks to "get an education which will make our people produce jobs for self and will make our people willing and able to go and do for self" (p. 39). Undergirding this education was the knowledge of self. The knowledge of self would stimulate ideas that would lead to the building of a new world.

The ideas for a new world were buried in the human being, and this led him to say the wisdom of God lives in us (E. Muhammad, 1974). The job of the teacher is to bring to life the wisdom of God that is asleep in the human being. Therefore, he taught about the foods to eat, which is a component of one's culture. He told his students to give up intoxicating drinks, tobacco products, and recreational drugs.

He admonished his students to pick up the intoxicating cup that Jesus asked his disciples to drink from, a cup that represents striving to live in unison with God's laws and commandments. This in turn would produce a new civilization. The people in that new civilization would not live to buy material things; they would be striving to ascertain the higher values that called their lives into existence. The education of Blacks in America should begin in all-Black school settings:

Education for my people should be where our children are off to them-selves for the first 15 or 16 years in classes separated by sex. Then they could and should seek higher education without the danger of losing respect for self or seeking to lose their identity. No people strive to lose themselves among other people except the so-called American Negroes. This they do because of their lack of knowledge of self. (E. Muhammad, 1965, p. 39)

In schools today, the identity of Black students in many cases instills in them a Eurocentric view of the world. Hilliard (1995) wrote,

More and more African Americans seem to be more and more confused about who they are. There is less of a deep sense of belonging to one's people. This not surprising. There is precious little in the society to teach African American children about themselves. (pp. 132–133)

The education of Blacks in America, according to Elijah Muhammad, should create a unity among them. However, to the contrary, those with PhDs can become vicious toward one another, never realizing their education missed the mark by not instilling unity among them as an oppressed people.

Hilliard (1995) wrote, "Real, self-destructive behavior occurs when we identify so strongly with our oppressors that we do to ourselves the worst that they could do to us" (p. 129). The self-destructive behav-iors that have been socially engineered to produce a culture foreign to Blacks in America can be eradicated by looking anew at the teachings of Elijah Muhammad.

Popular culture artists, at the behest of powerful record label execu-tives, are glorifying savagery and bestiality (W. Muhammad, 2017). However, through reflection and action, these popular culture art-ists could radically change the world by way of Elijah Muhammad's teachings.

This, in turn, would cause them to become the Five Percenters who teach wisdom, knowledge, and understanding to the masses. Elijah Muhammad's teaching was soul crafting and the making of a new human being, one who would be educated beyond the reptilian brain into the original man who gave birth to an entire universe.

References

Abdullah, J. (2016). Bismillah—message to the Blackman revisited: Being and power. In J. Conyers & A. Pitre (Eds.), *Africana Islamic studies* (pp. 43–58). Lexington.

Akbar, N. (1998). *Know thy self.* Mind Productions & Associates.

Akom, A. (2003). Reexamining resistance as oppositional behavior: The Nation of Islam and the creation of a Black achievement ideology. *Sociology of Education, 76*(4), 305–325.

Alexander, M. (2012). *The new Jim Crow: Mass incarceration in the age of colorblindness.* The New Press.

Allah, W. (2007). *In the name of Allah: A history of Clarence 13X and the Five Percenters.* A-Team Publishing.

Angelis, T. D. (1998). *Louis Farrakhan.* Chelsea House Publishers.

Apple, M. (2019). *Ideology and curriculum* (4th ed.). Routledge.

Aptheker, H., & Du Bois, W. E. B. (1973). *Annotated bibliography of the published writings of W. E. B. Du Bois.* Kraus-Thomson Organization.

Asante, M. K. (1991). The Afrocentric idea in education. *Journal of Negro Education, 60*(2), 170–179.

Asante, M. K. (2005). *Race, rhetoric, and identity: The architecton of soul.* Humanity Books.

Asante, M. K. (2017). *Revolutionary pedagogy: Primer for teachers of Black children.* Universal Write Publications.

Balk, A., & Haley, A. (1963, January 26). The Black merchants of hate. *Saturday Evening Post.* https://alexhaley.com/2018/08/06/black-merchants-of-hate.

Banks, J. A. (1972). *Black self-concept.* McGraw-Hill.

Banks, J. A. (2014). *An introduction to multicultural education* (5th ed.). Pearson.

Banks, J. A. (2019). *An introduction to multicultural education* (6th ed.). Pearson.

Bell, D. (1992). *Faces at the bottom of the well: The permanence of racism.* Basic Books.

Bentley, L. (1999, December). A brief biography of Paulo Freire. Pedagogy & Theatre of the Oppressed. https://ptoweb.org/aboutpto/a-brief-biography-of-paulo-freire.

Berg, H. (2009). *Elijah Muhammad and Islam.* New York University Press.

Berliner, D., & Biddle, B. (1995). *The manufactured crisis: Myths, fraud, and the attacks on America's public schools.* Basic Books.

Beynon, E. (1938). The voodoo cult among Negro migrants in Detroit. *American Journal of Sociology, 43*(6), 894–907. http://www.jstor.org/stable/2768686.

Bowles, S., & Gintis, H. (1976). *Schooling in capitalist America: Educational reform and the contradictions of economic life.* Basic Books.

Breitman, G. (Ed.). (1965). *Malcolm X speaks: Selected speeches and statements.* Merit Publishers.

Brooks, J. S., & Theoharis, G. (2018). *Whiteucation: Privilege, power, and prejudice in school and society.* Routledge.

Brown, L. (2021, May 24). UK BLM leader shot in head after "numerous death threats," party says. *New York Post.* https://nypost.com/2021/05/24/uk-blm-leader-sasha-johnson-shot-in-head-party-says.

Chiwanza, T. H. (2017, September 12). "The most important weapon in the hands of the oppressor is the mind of the oppressed"—Steve Biko. *The African Exponent.* https://www.africanexponent.com/post/8569-steve-biko-was-a-prominent-and-eminent-activist-in-the-fight-against-apartheid.

Clark, C., & O'Donnell, J. (Eds.). (1999). *Becoming and unbecoming White: Owning and disowning a racial identity.* Bergin & Garvey.

Clegg, C. (1997). *An original man: The life and times of Elijah Muhammad.* St. Martin's Press.

Cone, J. (2010). *A Black theology of liberation.* Oribis Books (original work published 1970).

Conyers, J. (Ed.). (2007). *Engines of the Black power movement: Essays on the influence of civil rights actions, arts, and Islam.* McFarland Publishers.

Conyers, J. (Ed.). (2017). *Molefi Kete Asante—a critical Afrocentric reader.* Peter Lang Publishing.

Conyers, J., & Pitre, A. (Eds.). (2016). *Africana Islamic Studies.* Lexington Books.

Cooper, W. (2019). *Behold a pale horse.* Light Technology Publishing (original work published 1991).

Crawford, M. (2015). *Black Muslims and the law: Civil liberties from Elijah Muhammad to Muhammad Ali.* Lexington Books.

CROE TV. (2018, August 17). Muhammad and friends live stream (A577) [video]. YouTube. https://www.youtube.com/watch?v=GLsn0hES468.

Cunningham, P. (2018, February 5). In keynote address, Cornel West urges integrity, action, and soulcraft. *Yale News*. https://news.yale.edu/2018/02/05/keynote-address-cornel-west-urges-integrity-action-and-soulcraft.

Curtis, E. E. (2006). *Black Muslim religion in the Nation of Islam, 1960–1975*. University of North Carolina Press.

Darder, A. (2015). *Freire and education*. Routledge.

Darder, A., Torres, R., & Baltodano, M. (Eds.). (2017). *The critical pedagogy reader* (3rd ed.). Routledge.

Darrah, N. (2018, February 6). Charleston Black Lives Matter leader shot, killed in New Orleans, niece says. *Fox News*. https://www.foxnews.com/us/charleston-black-lives-matter-leader-shot-killed-in-new-orleans-niece-says.

Delgado, R., & Stefancic, J. (2017). *Critical race theory: An introduction* (3rd ed.). New York University Press.

Dhaliwal, J. (2015, March 21). Hypocrisy is democracy. *I Am Hip-Hop*. https://www.iamhiphopmagazine.com/knowledge-session-democracy-is-hypocrisy-by-malcolm-x.

Diangelo, R. (2018). *White fragility: Why it's so hard for White people to talk about racism*. Beacon.

Du Bois, W. E. B. (1903). *The souls of Black folk*. A. C. McClurg & Co.

Ekiye, R. (2013, October 25). Farrakhan speaks on Malcolm X's separation from the Honorable Elijah Muhammad 5/6 [video]. YouTube. https://www.youtube.com/watch?v=0na56zzPqjI.

Esmail, A., & Pitre, A. (Eds.). (2018). *Research studies on educating for diversity and social justice*. Rowman & Littlefield.

Esmail, A., Pitre, A., & Aragon, A. (2017). *Perspectives on diversity, equity, and social justice in educational leadership*. Rowman & Littlefield.

Essien-Udom, E. U. (1962). *Black nationalism: A search for identity in America*. University of Chicago Press.

Evanzz, K. (2001). *The messenger: The rise and fall of Elijah Muhammad*. Vintage.

Fardan, D. (2001). *Yakub and the origins of White supremacy: Message to the White man & woman in America*. Lushena Books.

Farrakhan, L. (1989, October 24). International press conference. Nation of Islam. https://www.noi.org/oct-24-1989-press-conference.

Farrakhan, L. (1992, August 15). Why we must control the education of our children [speech]. *Final Call*. https://www.finalcall.com/columns/mlf-education.html.

Farrakhan, L. (1993). *Torchlight for America*. FCN Press.

Farrakhan, L. (2006). *Education is the key*. FCN Publishing.

Farrakhan, L. (2009). *The education challenge: A new educational paradigm for the 21st century*. Final Call.

Farrakhan, L. (2012). The true meaning of education. *Final Call*. http://www
.finalcall.com/artman/publish/Minister_Louis_Farrakhan_9/article_8731
.shtml.

Farrakhan, L. (2020). *The criterion* [video]. Nation of Islam. https://www.noi
.org/the-criterion.

Felber, G. (2020). *Those who know don't say: The Nation of Islam, the Black
freedom movement, and the carceral state*. University of North Carolina
Press.

Fine, K. (2019, March 26). GHS principal to White teachers: Check
your privilege. *New Old North*. https://newoldnorth.com/2019/03/26/
ghs-principal-to-white-teachers-check-your-privilege.

Freire, P. (2018). *Pedagogy of the oppressed*. Bloomsbury Academic (original
work published 1968).

Gardell, M. (1996). *In the name of Elijah Muhammad: Louis Farrakhan and
the Nation of Islam*. Duke University Press.

Gatto, J. T. (2017). *Dumbing us down: The hidden curriculum of compulsory
schooling*. New Society Publishers.

Gibson, D., & Berg, H. (Eds.). (2016). *New perspectives on the Nation of Islam*.
Routledge.

Giroux, H. (2010, October 17). Lessons from Paulo Freire. *Chronicle of Higher
Education, 57*(9).

Giroux, H. (2020). *On critical pedagogy* (2nd ed.). Bloomsbury.

Gollnick, D. M., & Chinn, P. C. (2017). *Multicultural education in a pluralistic
society* (10th ed.). Pearson.

Greenleaf, R. K. (n.d.). *What is servant leadership?* Robert K. Greenleaf
Center for Servant Leadership. https://www.greenleaf.org/what-is-servant
-leadership.

Gregory, D. (2016, May 28). *Dick Gregory on Malcolm X's assassination*
[video]. YouTube. https://youtu.be/y7i3XTHrUxo.

Haberman, M. (1991). The pedagogy of poverty versus good teaching. *Phi
Delta Kappan, 73*(4), 290–294.

Hakim, I. (n.d.). *I bear witness: Nation of Islam theology from a Caucasian
viewpoint*. Ida Hakim.

Hakim, N. (1997). *The black stone: The true history of Elijah Muhammad:
Messenger of Allah*. M.E.M.P.S. Publications.

Halasa, M. (1990). *Elijah Muhammad: Religious leader*. Chelsea House
Publishers.

Haley, A. (1965). *The autobiography of Malcolm X*. Ballentine Books.

Haley, A., & Balks, A. (1963, January 26). The Black merchants of hate.
Saturday Evening Post.

Hilliard, A. (1995). *The maroon within us: Selected essays on African American community socialization*. Black Classic Press.

Hine, D., Hine, W., & Harrold, S. (2009). *African Americans: A concise history* (3rd ed.). Pearson.

History.com Editors. (2018, September 12). *Muhammad Ali*. History.com. https://www.history.com/topics/black-history/muhammad-ali.

Howard, G. (2006). *We can't teach what we don't know: White teachers in multiracial schools*. Teachers College Press.

Howard, T. (2020). *Why race and culture matter in schools: Closing the achievement gap in America's classrooms* (2nd ed.). Teachers College Press.

Ignatiev, N., & Garvey, J. (1996). *Race traitor*. Routledge.

Illich, I. (1971). *De-schooling society*. Harper.

Janson, M. (2016). Unity through diversity: A case study of Chrislam in Lagos. *Africa: Journal of the International African Institute, 86*(4), 646–672.

Jeffries, B. (2014). *A nation can rise no higher than its women: African American Muslim women in the movement for Black self-determination, 1950–1975*. Lexington Books.

Kamiya, G. (2017, February 7) How red-baiting crusade collapsed in SF court-room in 1960. San Francisco Chronicle.

Karenga, M. (2002). *An introduction to Black studies* (3rd ed). University of Sankore Press.

Karenga, M. (2007). Us, Kawaida and the Black liberation movement in the 1960's: Culture, knowledge and struggle. In J. Conyers (Ed.), *Engines of the Black power movement: Essays on the influence of civil rights actions, arts, and Islam* (pp. 95–133). McFarland.

Khan, M. Y. (1959, August 15). White man is God cult of Islam. *New Crusader*.

Khan, S. J. (2014, July 26). Prophet Muhammad (saw)'s call to prophethood. *Muslim Times*. https://themuslimtimes.info/2014/07/26/prophet-muhammad -saws-first-call-to-prophethood.

Kincheloe, J. (2008). *Critical pedagogy: A primer* (2nd ed.). Peter Lang.

King, J. E. (2015). *Dysconscious racism, Afrocentric praxis, and education for human freedom: Through the years I keep on toiling—the selected works of Joyce King*. Routledge.

Kohli, R. (2009) Critical race reflections: Valuing the experiences of teachers of color in teacher education. *Race Ethnicity and Education, 12*(2), 235–251.

Ladson-Billings, G. (1995). But that's just good teaching! The case for cultur-ally relevant pedagogy. *Theory into Practice, 34*(3), 59–65.

Ladson-Billings, G. (Ed.). (2005) *Beyond the big house: African American educators on teacher education*. Teachers College Press.

Ladson-Billings, G. (2021). Fighting for our lives: Preparing teacher to teach African American students. In A. Pitre, T. Hudson, J. Smith-Gray, & K. James (Eds.), *The Gloria Ladson-Billings Reader* (pp. 172–184). Cognella.

Ladson-Billings, G., & Tate, W. (1995). Toward a critical race theory of educa-tion. *Teacher College Record, 97*(1), 47–68.

Leonardo, Z. (2009). The pale/ontology: The status of Whiteness in education. In M. Apple, W. Au, & L. Gandin (Eds.). *The Routledge international handbook on critical education* (pp. 23–126). Routledge.

Lincoln, C. E. (1960). *Black Muslims in America*. Duke University Press.

Lincoln, C. E. (1963). *The Black Muslims in America*. Beacon.

Lowen, J. (2007). *The lies my teacher told me: Everything your American history textbook got wrong*. New Press.

Malcolm X. (2019). History is a weapon. In A. Pitre (Ed.), *A critical Black pedagogy reader: The brothers speak* (pp. 61–67). Rowman & Littlefield.

Marable, M. (2011). *Malcolm X: A life of reinvention*. Viking.

Maslow, A. H. (1943). A theory of human motivation. *Psychological Review, 50*(4), 370–396.

Maxwell, J. (1998). *The 21 irrefutable laws of leadership*. Thomas Nelson.

McIntosh, P. (1998). *White privilege: Unpacking the invisible knapsack*. In M. McGoldrick (Ed.), *Re-visioning family therapy: Race, culture, and gender in clinical practice* (pp. 147–152). Guilford Press.

McLaren, P. (2015). *Life in schools: An introduction to critical pedagogy in the foundations of education* (6th ed.). Routledge.

Montgomery, E. (1963, July 28). Black Muslim founder exposed as White. *Los Angeles Evening Herald-Examiner*.

Muhammad, B. (2002). *Dear holy apostle: Experiences and letters of guidance with the honorable Elijah Muhammad*. Ashanti Enterprises.

Muhammad, D. (2020). *But, didn't you kill Malcolm? Myth busting the propaganda against the Nation of Islam*. Research Minister.

Muhammad, E. (1965). *Message to the Blackman in America*. Final Call.

Muhammad, E. (1967). *How to eat to live*. M.E.M.P.S. Publications.

Muhammad, E. (1973). *The fall of America*. Final Call.

Muhammad, E. (1974). *Our savior has arrived*. Final Call.

Muhammad, E. (1992). *The theology of time*. United Brothers Communications Systems.

Muhammad, E. (1993a). *Christianity vs. Islam*. M.E.M.P.S. Publications.

Muhammad, E. (1993b). *History of the Nation of Islam*. Secretarius M.E.M.P.S. Publications.

Muhammad, E. (1993c). *Supreme wisdom*. Final Call.

Muhammad, E. (1993d). *Birth of a saviour*. Coalition for the Remembrance of Elijah Muhammad (CROE).

Muhammad, E. (1997). *The science of time: The time and judgment—when self tells the truth on self*. M.E.M.P.S. Publications.

Muhammad, E. (2002). *The God-science of Black power*. Secretarius M.E.M.P.S. Publications (original speech from 1967).

Muhammad, E. (2006). *The theology of time*. M.E.M.P.S. Publications.

Muhammad, E. (2012). *Ministry class taught by Elijah Muhammad in the 1930s*. Medina Mohammad.

Muhammad, E. (2019, July 16). Every time you look at a Black man you're looking at God [Video]. YouTube. https://youtu.be/GVyuTUso9Y8.

Muhammad, J. (1996). *This is the one: The most honored Elijah Muhammad, we need not look for another* (3rd ed.). Book Company.

Muhammad, J. (2012, October 28). Is it possible that the honorable Elijah Muhammad is still physically alive??? *Final Call*. http://www.finalcall.com/artman/publish/Columns_4/article_9318.shtml.

Muhammad, J. (2020, January 14). Measuring and closing the gap. *Final Call*. https://www.finalcall.com/artman/publish/Columns_4/Measuring_and_closing_the_gap_by_Jabril_Muhammad_3071.shtml.

Muhammad, R. (2013). *UFO's and the Nation of Islam: The source, proof, and reality of the wheels*. Nation Brothers.

Muhammad, R. (2016, June 19). *Made by Elijah: Farrakhan speaks on the life and times of Muhammad Ali*. *Final Call*. https://www.finalcall.com/artman/publish/National_News_2/article_103160.shtml.

Muhammad, S. (2003). *How to teach math to Black students*. African American Images.

Muhammad, S. (2012). *Table talks of the honorable Elijah Muhammad*. MUI Press.

Muhammad, T. (2021a, February 23). Dr Wesley Muhammad talks Malcolm X and the wives of the Messenger . . . and the three violations & more [video]. YouTube. https://www.youtube.com/watch?v=1oD7fLzMsSU.

Muhammad, T. (2021b, March 16). To return is turning and evolving on the sacred path of Allah, God's love, peace and happiness! *Final Call*. https://new.finalcall.com/2021/03/16/to-return-is-turning-and-evolving-on-the-sacred-path-of-allah-goda-love-peace-and-happiness.

Muhammad, T. (2021c, March 21). We have come to the end of the old mind and old world's thinking as we enter the changeover of worlds. *Final Call*. https://new.finalcall.com/2021/03/02/we-have-come-to-the-end-of-the-old-mind-and-the-old-worlda-s-thinking-as-we-enter-the-changeover-of-worlds.

Muhammad, W. (2017). *Understanding the assault on the Black man, Black manhood and Black masculinity*. A-Team Publishing.

Muhammad, W. (2019, March 11). *Master W. Fard Muhammad and FBI COINTELPRO*. Nation of Islam. https://www.noi.org/fard-muhammad-fbi-cointelpro.

Muhammad, Z. (2020). *Mother of the nation Clara Evans Muhammad: Wife of Elijah Muhammad, mother of Imam W. Deen Mohammed*. Institute of Muslim American Studies.

Muhammad-Ali, J. (2002). *The evolution of the Nation of Islam: The story of the Honorable Elijah Muhammad*. JMA Pub.

Newberg, A. (2010). *The principles of neurotheology.* Ashgate.

Newberg, A., & Waldman, M. R. (2009). *How God changes your brain: Breakthrough findings from a leading neuroscientist.* Ballantine Books.

Nieto, S., & Bode, P. (2018). *Affirming diversity: The sociopolitical context of multicultural education.* Pearson.

Norment, N. (2019). *African American studies: The discipline and its dimensions.* Peter Lang.

Ooyiman. (2020, September 6). *The honorable Elijah Muhammad is physically alive* [video]. YouTube. https://www.youtube.com/watch?v=kmJ7D3JP74U.

Owino, A. (2019, January 3). Pio Gama Pinto inspired Malcolm X to carry on activism. Kenyans.co.ke. https://www.kenyans.co.ke/news/35699-pio-gama-pinto-inspired-malcolm-x-carry-activism.

Oxman, R. (2017, March 26). Securing sweetness for sugarcane souls: A tribute to Paulo Freire. *Countercurrents.* https://countercurrents.org/2017/04/securing-sweetness-for-sugarcane-souls-a-tribute-to-paulo-freire.

Ozmon, H., & Craver, S. (2008). *Philosophical foundations of education* (8th ed.). Pearson Prentice Hall.

Payne, L., & Payne, T. (2021). *The dead are rising: The life of Malcolm X.* Liveright Publishing Corporation.

Person-Lynn, K. (1996). *First word: Black scholars, thinkers, warriors.* Harlem River Press.

Picower, B., & Kohli, R. (2017). *Confronting racism in teacher education: Counternarratives of critical practice.* Routledge.

Pinar, W. (2005). The problem with curriculum and pedagogy. *Journal of Curriculum and Pedagogy, 2*(1), 62–87.

Pinar, W. (2020). *What is curriculum theory* (3rd ed.). Routledge.

Pipes, D. (2000). How Elijah Muhammad won. Daniel Pipes Middle East Forum. http://www.danielpipes.org/article/341.

Pitre, A. (2011). *Freedom fighters: The struggle instituting Black history in K-12 education.* Cognella.

Pitre, A. (2015). *The educational philosophy of Elijah Muhammad: Education for a new world* (3rd ed.). Hamilton Books.

Pitre, A. (2016). Introduction. In J. Conyers and A. Pitre (Eds.), *Africana Islamic studies.* Lexington Books.

Pitre, A. (2018). *Farrakhan and education* (2nd ed.). Cognella.

Pitre, A. (2019). *A critical Black pedagogy reader: The brothers speak.* Rowman & Littlefield.

Pitre, A. (2021a). *An introduction to Elijah Muhammad studies: The new educational paradigm.* Hamilton Books.

Pitre, A. (2021b). *An introduction to Elijah Muhammad studies: The new educational paradigm* (Rev. ed.). Hamilton Books.

Pitre, A. (2021c). *Elijah Muhammad—original man know thyself: A pedagogy for Black liberation.* Cognella.

Pitre, A., & Hudson, T. (2020). Educating for social justice: The potential role of historically Black colleges and universities in the 21st century. In J. Conyers, C. Edwards, & K. Thompson (Eds.), *African Americans in higher education: A critical study of social and philosophical foundations of Africana culture* (pp. 51–66). Meyers Education Press.

Pitre, A., Hudson, T., Smith-Gray, J., & James, K. (Eds.). (2021). *The Gloria Ladson-Billings reader.* Cognella.

Pitre, A., & Smith-Gray, J. (2020). Preparing educational leaders for social justice: The case of historically Black colleges and universities. In R. Papa (Ed.), *Handbook on promoting social justice in education* (pp. 1899–1912). Springer. https://link.springer.com/content/pdf/10.1007/978-3-030-14625-2_85.pdf.

Rabaka, R. (2006). Africana critical theory of contemporary society: The role of radical politics, social theory, and Africana philosophy. In M. K. Asante & M. Karenga (Eds.), *Handbook of Black studies* (pp. 130–151). SAGE.

Rashad, A. (2019). *Islam, Black nationalism, and slavery: A detailed history.* Writers Inc.

RemembranceOfAllah. (1992/2012). Historic interview with Imam Warith Deen Mohammed [video]. YouTube. https://www.youtube.com/watch?v=TAC3d9aqm9k.

Safir, S. (2020, December 2). Before Maslow's hierarchy: The whitewashing of indigenous knowledge. Shane Safir. https://shanesafir.com/2020/12/before-maslows-hierarchy-the-whitewashing-of-indigenous-knowledge.

Sahib, H. (1951). The Nation of Islam. *Contributions in Black Studies, 13*(1), https://scholarworks.umass.edu/cibs/vol13/iss1/3.

Shabazz, B. (Ed.). (1967). *Malcolm X on Afro-American history.* Pathfinder.

Shah, Z. H. (2014, March 9). The earliest biography of Muhammad, by ibn Ishaq / ibn Hisham. *Muslim Times.* https://themuslimtimes.info/2014/03/09/the-earliest-biography-of-muhammad-by-ibn-ishaq-ibn-hisham.

Sleeter, C. (2004). How White teachers construct race. In G. Ladson-Billings & D. Gillborn (Eds.), *The Routledge Falmer reader in multicultural education* (pp. 163–178). Routledge.

Sleeter, C., & Grant, C. (2009). *Making choices for multicultural education: Five approaches to race, class and gender* (6th ed.). Wiley.

Smith, L. (2012). Decolonizing methodologies: Research and indigenous peoples (2nd ed.). Zed Books.

Southern Poverty Law Center (SPLC). (2021). Antisemitism. SPLC. https://www.splcenter.org/fighting-hate/extremist-files/ideology/antisemitism.

Spivey, D. (2007). *Schooling for the new slavery: Black industrial education, 1868–1915.* Africa World Press.

Spring, J. H. (2011). *The politics of American education.* Routledge.

Spring, J. H. (2016). *Deculturalization and the struggle for equality: Brief history of the education of dominated cultures in the United States.* Routledge.

Stevens, C. (2012, February 6). Paulo Freire. Critical Pedagogy on the Web. https://web.archive.org/web/20120206062445/http://mingo.info-science .uiowa.edu/~stevens/critped/freire.htm.

StreamingChurch Archives. (2018, December 26). Munir Muhammad Show (MM2234) [Video]. YouTube. https://www.youtube.com/watch?v =NTSrONV_ZsU&t=54s.

Taylor, U. (2017). *The promise of patriarchy: Women in the Nation of Islam.* University of North Carolina Press.

The Famous People. (n.d.). Muhammad Ali biography. The Famous People. https://www.thefamouspeople.com/profiles/muhammad-ali-2411.php.

Toure, K., & Hamilton, C. (1992). *Black power: The politics of liberation in America.* Vintage Press.

Townsend, S., Osmond, G., & Phillips, M. (2018). "Where Cassius Clay ends, Muhammad Ali begins": Sportspeople, political activism, and methodology. *International Journal of the History of Sport, 35*(11), 1149–1175.

Truth/Controversy. (2020, May 16). Hon. Elijah Muhammad–Buzz Anderson interview 1964 [video]. YouTube. https://www.youtube.com/watch?v =5tTU9m5G7vk&t=19s.

Turner, N. (2019, January 10). A passport to the future. The Raising Supaman Project. https://raisingsupaman.com/2019/01/a-passport-to-the-future.

University of Southern California, School of International Relations. (n.d.) USCDornsife. https://dornsife.usc.edu.

Walker, D. (2005). *Islam and the search for African American nationhood: Elijah Muhammad, Louis Farrakhan, and the Nation of Islam.* Clarity Press.

Wallace, M., & Lomax, L. (1959, July 13–17). *The hate that hate produced* [five-part docuseries]. Distributed by WNTA-TV.

Watkins, W. (2001). *The White architects of Black education: Ideology and power in America, 1865–1954.* Teachers College Press.

Welsing, F. (1991). *The Isis papers: Keys to color.* Third World Press.

Woodson, C. G. (1999). *The mis-education of the Negro* (11th ed.). First Africa World Press (original work published 1933).

Zeringue, N. (2021, March 12). Opelousas High teacher charged for battery of student wearing "Black Lives Matter" hoodie. *KLFY News.* https://www .klfy.com/st-landry-parish/opelousas-high-teacher-charged-for-battery-of -student-wearing-black-lives-matter-hoodie.

Zirin, D. (2017, April 24). "Sports Illustrated" gets everything about Muhammad Ali and Malcolm X wrong. *The Nation.* https://www.thenation.com/ article/archive/sports-illustrated-gets-everything-about-muhammad-ali-and -malcolm-x-wrong.

Index

achievement gap, 33, 65
acquisition of knowledge, 23–24,
   91, 98
Africana Islamic Studies (Conyers,
   Pitre), 21
African Americans. *See* Black
   people
Africana studies, 11, 61, 63, 96
African-centered historical
   perspectives, 28, 35, 59, 67, 84,
   92; in CBP, 61, 66, 87
African holocaust, 76
Afrocentrism, 22, 108
agriculture, 58–59
Ali, Muhammad (Cassius Clay), 12,
   51–52, 84, 86–87; as pupil of
   Muhammad, E., 96–98
Allah. *See* God
Anderson, Buzz, 59
anti-Black racism, 27, 76
antiracism, 6
Apple, Michael, 14, 39–40
arrests, 46, 48, 60; of Muhammad,
   E., 11, 24, 47, 53, 93–94
artificial intelligence, 32, 43
Asante, Molefi, 29, 66, 108

assassination, of Malcolm X, 18, 92;
   Muhammad, E., blamed for, 17,
   50–51, 54
astronomy, 57, 68–69, 81
awakening, spiritual, xiii–xv, 4, 8,
   62–63. *See also* soul crafting

Bahar, Wali, 51
Banks, James, 22–23, 66, 70
Becoming and Unbecoming White
   (Clark, O'Donnell), 77
Bell, Derrick, xiv, 30, 71
Berg, Herbert, 21
Berry, Henry, 53
Beynon, Edmond, 19, 30
Bible, 44, 74, 84, 102–3; Jesus in,
   64, 79; Muhammad, E., on, 40,
   41, 43–44; names, 24, 38–39; as
   tool of oppression, 38
Biko, Steven, 54
bin Naufal, Waraqa, 25–26
Black consciousness, x, 8, 13, 15,
   73–75, 83–84, 104, 108
Black education, 4–6, 8, 15, 38–40,
   53, 61, 104; knowledge of self
   missing in, 64–65; labor and, 58

power, 29, 61, 101, 102; of
  education, 7, 9; of thought, 9–10
prisons, 21, 47–48, 87, 94
privilege, White, 7
propaganda, xii, 30, 31, 51. *See also*
  false narratives
property, 3, 36–37, 58–59; enslaved
  people as, 36, 71–72
Prossey, Gabriel, 38
protests, xi, 39
public pedagogy, 68
public schools, ix–x, 2, 13, 24, 48,
  53, 105; Black history missing in,
  73; desegregation of, 75; Giroux
  on, 63
pupils of Muhammad, E., xii, 12, 52,
  86–88; Ali as, 96–98; Farrakhan
  as, 68, 71, 98–101; Malcolm
  X as, xiv–xv, 24, 71, 89–93;
  Mohammad, Imam Warith Deen,
  as, 93–96

Quran, 4, 24–25, 32, 47–48, 80, 84,
  103–4

Rabaka, Reiland, 61
race, 23, 57, 73, 102; in the Bible,
  38–39
Race Traitor (Ignatiev, Garvey),
  76–77
racism, 6–7, 13–14, 23–24, 61, 73,
  99; of high-stakes testing, 5, 33,
  65, 85; Muhammad, E., accused
  of, xi, 81, 102; reverse, 58, 84,
  102
Rahman, Abdul (Captain Sam X), 96
reading. *See* literacy/reading
real estate, property as, 36, 72
reeducation program, xi, 22, 24, 29,
  62–63, 84, 86, 97
religions, 3, 7–8, 22–26, 28–29. *See
  also specific religions*

religious diversity, 32, 43
reverse racism, 58, 84, 102
Revolutionary Pedagogy (Asante), 29
rights, 8, 21, 27
ruling society (Western-centric), 58,
  65, 78, 107–8; Christianity of,
  22–26, 38–39; knowledge hidden
  by, 2–3, 5, 39–40, 53

Sahib, Hatim, 19–20, 44–45, 47
Satan, 80
Savior's Day Convention, Nation of
  Islam, 50, 52, 99
Sedalia, North Carolina, 11, 104
self-autopoiesis, 64
self-destructive behaviors, 4, 104,
  109
self-determination, 61, 92
separationism, 13, 27–28
separation of church and state, 40, 63
September 11, 2001 attacks, 23, 31
servant leadership, 84, 88
Shabazz, Malik El Hajj. *See* X,
  Malcolm
sharecroppers, xiv, 41, 45, 52, 86
skin color, 22, 23–24, 44, 78, 90
slave owners/slave masters, 8, 13,
  36–37, 40, 71, 75
slavery/enslaved people, 25, 38, 44;
  chattel, 3–4, 9, 12–13 14, 23;
  citizenship status of, 35, 107;
  literacy prohibited for, 12–13, 37;
  as property, 36, 71–72
Sleeter, C., 26, 33–34
Smith, L., 34
social engineering, 10, 68
social justice, 18, 26–30, 58; in field
  of education, 13–14, 31
soul crafting, xiii, xv, 9, 13, 83–86,
  97, 106–9
the South, U.S., 41–42, 45, 75, 86,
  88–89

Watkins, William, 5–6, 28
weaponization, 10, 50; of education, 33, 65, 85
We Can't Teach What We Don't Know (Howard), 38
Welsing, Frances, 39
West, Cornell, xv, 86
"What to the Slave Is the Fourth of July" speech, 35
The White Architects of Black Education (Watkins), 28
White Fragility (Diangelo), 27
White men, 35, 36
Whiteness, 13–14, 22, 30, 39, 71, 76–78
Whiteness studies, xiii, xiv, 76–80
White people, 27; origins of, 23, 77–80, 85; as slave masters, 8, 13, 36–37, 40, 71
White Privilege (McIntosh), 67
White students, 65, 105
White supremacy, 22, 33, 37, 61; Black people internalizing, 6, 27; Christianity supporting, 38–39; ideology of, 24, 28, 38, 67

White teachers, 26, 33, 67; Black students experiences with, ix–x, 7, 34, 89–90, 98–99
Whiteucation (Brooks, Theoharis), 80
White women, 7, 44
Winston Salem Teachers College, 99
wives, 25–26, 49–50, 54
women, xv, 106; White, 7, 44
Woodson, Carter G., ix–x, 6–7, 9, 26–27, 33, 61, 65, 96; on Black education, 40

X, Malcolm (Malcolm Little), x, 8, 13, 81, 83, 96, 99; assassination of, 17–18, 50–51, 54, 92; on names, 37; as pupil of Muhammad, E., xiv–xv, 24, 71, 89–93; suspension from Nation of Islam of, 48–49

Yahweh. *See* God
Yakub (White men originating from), 77–78, 80
yellow journalism, 30, 50
Yoruba people, 15

Made in the USA
Las Vegas, NV
30 August 2022

54410511R00090